"It is fortunate that this book is so well written, because it should be required reading for all who are engaged in the helping professions, as well as for all who are committed to caring."

M. Scott Peck, M.D., author of *The Road Less Traveled*

~

"This book is meta-service: service to the servers. It has the pulse of heart within heart."

Stewart Brand, *Whole Earth Review*

~

"A perfect resource for volunteers who want to examine their work more closely. This is a remarkable book—one that challenges us to understand the impact of our efforts to help, not only on our communities, but on us as helpers and as people with needs."

Kerry Kenn Allen, President of VOLUNTEER—
The National Center

~

"A truly glorious book which is a must for anyone in the field of service. It puts us in touch with what trust and unconditional love are all about—both for our fellow man as well as for ourselves. The stories in this book are beautiful examples of living humanity."

Elisabeth Kübler-Ross, author of *On Death and Dying*

Also by Ram Dass

Be Here Now (*1971*)

The Only Dance There Is (*1974*)

Grist for the Mill (*1977*)

Journey of Awakening (*1978*)

Miracle of Love (*1979*)

HOW
CAN
I
HELP?

HOW
CAN
I
HELP?

*Stories and Reflections
on Service*

Ram Dass

and

Paul Gorman

ALFRED A. KNOPF NEW YORK 2001

Grateful acknowledgment is made to the following for permission to reprint previously published material:
Terry Dobson: for the story on p. 167. Copyright © 1981 Terry Dobson. Reprinted by permission of Terry Dobson.

Thich Nhat Hanh: for the poem "Please Call Me by My True Names" on p. 178. Copyright © 1983 Thich Nhat Hanh. Reprinted by permission of Thich Nhat Hanh.

Harper & Row, Publishers, Inc.: for the excerpt on p. 12, from p. 35 of The Way of Life According to Lao Tzu translated by Witter Bynner (John Day). Copyright 1944 by Witter Bynner. Reprinted by permission of Harper & Row, Publishers, Inc.

Chet Manchester: for the story on p. 212. Reprinted by permission of Chet Manchester.

Random House, Inc.: for the excerpt on p. 60 from "Musée des Beaux Arts" from W. H. Auden: Collected Poems, edited by Edward Mendelson. Copyright 1940 and renewed 1968 by W. H. Auden. Reprinted by permission of Random House, Inc.

Simon & Schuster, Inc.: for the story on p. 117 from Mortal Lessons by Richard Selzer. Copyright © 1974, 1975, 1976 by Richard Selzer. Reprinted by permission of Simon & Schuster, Inc.

Whatever Publishing, Inc.: for the story on p. 3 from The Dolphons' Gift by Elizabeth Gawain. Copyright © 1981 by Elizabeth Gawain, pp. 233–4. Reprinted by permission of Whatever Publishing, Inc., Mill Valley, California.

Library of Congress Cataloging in Publication Data
Ram Dass.
    How can I help?
    1. Helping behavior. I. Gorman, Paul, 1940–
II. Title.
BF637.H4R36 1985 158 84-48734
ISBN 0-394-72947-1

Cover design by Sara Eisenman

Manufactured in the United States of America
Published April 22, 1985
Reprinted Fifteen Times
Seventeenth Printing, October 2001

Acknowledgments

It was out of the Seva Foundation that the initial impetus for this book arose. The foundation, which was created as a vehicle for compassionate service, saw as one of its functions that of helping others find ways to serve, ways which would also be beneficial to the servers themselves. A book for a general audience, addressing the issues all of us face when called upon to care for one another, seemed a useful way to share the values that Seva represents.

As we began work on the book and we sought to identify issues to treat and individuals to talk to, it often seemed as if we were being sent on a treasure hunt, not knowing what wonderful person we would meet or story we would hear next. Many, many people—too many to enumerate—helped speed us along this journey. In the files of Voluntary Action Centers in several cities—agencies which place volunteers in service positions—we were able to locate a number of unsung heroes and heroines; we are indebted to these remarkable clearing houses of

Acknowledgments

good works. From the greater chorus of these voices we have been able to include only the words of a few. With their agreement, we have presented their accounts without attribution in the text. Here, we all felt, was a way to evoke the universality of experience and power of common wisdom which is so central a theme in the book. A number of people even requested anonymity. But there are those, who talked to us at length and whose accounts we have included in some detail, whom we can thank publicly: William Hirscher, Marie Rapello, Mischa Avramoff, Bill Donaldson, Wavy Gravy, Patricia Lowery, Robert Louden, Charles Piera, Larry and Girija Brilliant, Raphael Flores, Peggy Dillon, and Harriet Krasnoff. The inspiration of their example has remained with us long after the time we spent together.

Much shorter excerpts have come from conferences and broadcasts in which participants did not identify themselves by name but understood they were collaborators in our work and expressed willingness to have their remarks included. We thank them, and are especially grateful to Omega Institute in Rhinebeck, New York, and WBAI-FM in New York City, for hosting a number of particularly valuable meetings and conversations.

Lillian North assisted us by transcribing interviews and conferences. Enid Gorman was a steady source of perspective and good judgment. And to Toinette Lippe, our friend and editor, our deepest thanks for her faith in this project from the outset, her patience and emotional support, and her own very special understanding of the issues we have treated. To N. K. B., thank you.

Contents

Preface

This book began, in a sense, with people asking, "How can I help?" Sometimes the question was raised in specific circumstances: a woman concerned about her best friend's depression, a nurse wondering what she might offer patients in addition to medical care, someone with time on his hands, eager to be more useful. On other occasions broader political issues were the catalyst. Often the inquiry grew out of very personal introspection into what constitutes a good and happy life. It was asked of us individually, regarding projects in which we ourselves were directly involved. However, more often than not, we heard it as "something in the air," an open-ended question about people's relationship to one another and to human suffering in general.

"How can I help?" is a timeless inquiry of the heart. Yet we often heard it asked in the context of our own culture and moment. As commitment to service has ebbed and flowed, many of us have spent a great deal of time considering the deeper values of our helping work.

What exactly is the nature of conscious service? What are the challenges posed by present conditions? Our book grows out of this collective reflection.

As if to underscore the degree of shared concern, the book evolved into a wider collaboration than we had initially intended. "How can I help?" led us to investigate "How are we helping?" We met with many people active in the mainstream and tributaries of service and social action in America. What were the important issues they were encountering?

At a national conference of such organizations, one response came from an officer of Volunteer, the nation's largest umbrella organization for voluntary action centers and groups. "Recruitment, administration, publicity, funding, lobbying . . . we know something about all these. *But what really helps? Deep down, whatever we're doing, what really helps?"* His words resonated strongly with all assembled, and continue to do so in this book.

Our journey took us to workplaces, as well. We spent many hours listening to stories from those who face suffering and serve others, day in and night out. We discovered an extraordinarily deep pool of wisdom and compassion in so many different people: a doctor in an intensive care unit, an organizer of a church food drive for the homeless, a Rotary Club volunteer, a drug counselor, a peace activist, a stroke patient, a group of senior citizens in a community center basement. . . .

We found many of their accounts so moving that we resolved to include them as central elements of the book. What better way to remind ourselves of how much we all have to offer one another? Here, in effect, was one part of our answer to the question posed by the book's title.

Look to one another. Look to what we already know or have learned.

To these stories we have added our own reflections. Sometimes our impulse was simply to appreciate and ponder essential truths revealed by these tales; these were living parables. On other occasions, the testimonies helped us identify and examine specific challenges all of us face, caring for one another. Such movement from story to reflection may mirror the way we all live and work—now immersed in action, now stepping back to make sense of it all. Counterpoint, then, is the rhythm of this book, conversation its tone—a dialogue in which we now invite our readers to join.

Authors usually come to such an inquiry with a bias. We seem to have had several. One of us was trained in psychology, the other in philosophy. One has had experience as a therapist, the other in politics. Both of us have been deeply influenced by spiritual practice and the teachings of the world's religions, all of which emphasize service. We honor and draw from these traditions, although what we have to share should be accessible to those who follow none.

Many perspectives as well as many voices, then, sound through these pages. Perhaps this is appropriate, for it is our hope that this book might be useful to everyone. How much time, after all, does each and every one of us spend helping and being helped? The forms may vary: the helping professions, self-help groups, service as religious practice, movements for social change, voluntary service. A 1983 Gallup poll found that 55 percent of all Americans spend at least a few hours volunteering to assist neighbors and communities. But how could any poll measure common courtesies, thoughtful gestures, the simplest moments of human affirmation?

We have resolved to consider what is common to all these forms. Seeking to care for others, each of us inevitably faces certain fundamental challenges. These are what draw us to explore the very heart of helping. We offer this book, then, with great respect for the work each reader is already embarked upon.

HOW
CAN
I
HELP?

1
Natural Compassion

I was in about forty feet of water, alone. I knew I should not have gone alone, but I was very competent and just took a chance. There was not much current, and the water was so warm and clear and enticing. But when I got a cramp, I realized at once how foolish I was. I was not very alarmed, but was completely doubled up with stomach cramp. I tried to remove my weight belt, but I was so doubled up I could not get to the catch. I was sinking and began to feel more frightened, unable to move. I could see my watch and knew that there was only a little more time on the tank before I would be finished with breathing! I tried to massage my abdomen. I wasn't wearing a wet suit, but couldn't straighten out and couldn't get to the cramped muscles with my hands.

I thought, "I can't go like this! I have things to do!" I just couldn't die anonymously this way, with no one to even know what happened to me. I called out in my mind, "Somebody, something, help me!"

I was not prepared for what happened. Suddenly I felt a

prodding from behind me under the armpit. I thought, "Oh no, sharks!" I felt real terror and despair. But my arm was being lifted forcibly. Around into my field of vision came an eye—the most marvelous eye I could ever imagine. I swear it was smiling. It was the eye of a big dolphin. Looking into that eye, I knew I was safe.

It moved farther forward, nudging under, and hooked its dorsal fin under my armpit with my arm over its back. I relaxed, hugging it, flooded with relief. I felt that the animal was conveying security to me, that it was healing me as well as lifting me toward the surface. My stomach cramp went away as we ascended, and I relaxed with security, but I felt very strongly that it healed me too.

At the surface, it drew me all the way in to shore. It took me into water so shallow that I began to be concerned for it, that it would be beached, and I pushed it back a little deeper, where it waited, watching me, I guess to see if I was all right.

It felt like another lifetime. When I took off the weight belt and oxygen, I just took everything off and went naked back into the ocean to the dolphin. I felt so light and free and alive, and just wanted to play in the sun and the water, in all that freedom. The dolphin took me back out and played around in the water with me. I noticed that there were a lot of dolphins there, farther out.

After a while it brought me back to shore. I was very tired then, almost collapsing, and he made sure I was safe in the shallowest water. Then he turned sideways with one eye looking into mine. We stayed that way for what seemed like a very long time, timeless I guess, in a trance almost, with personal thoughts of the past going through my mind.

Then he made just one sound and went out to join the others, and all of them left.

~

At times, helping happens simply in the way of things. It's not something we really think about, merely the instinctive response of an open heart. Caring is a reflex. Someone slips, your arm goes out. A car is in a ditch, you join the others and push. A colleague at work has the blues, you let her know you care. It all seems natural and appropriate. You live, you help.

When we join together in this spirit, action comes more effortlessly, and everybody ends up nourished. Girding against the flood . . . setting up a community meeting . . . preparing a funeral . . . people seem to know their part. We sense what's called for, or if we don't, and feel momentarily awkward, someone comes quickly with an idea, and it's just right, and we're grateful. We baby-sit the kids while their parents move possessions to homes farther from the rising river . . . we bring a comfortable chair for an older person who might attend the meeting . . . we call the rabbi with a favorite psalm of the one who has just died. Needs are anticipated, and glances of appreciation among us are enough to confirm that it's all going well.

We take pleasure not only in what we did but in the way we did it. On the one hand, the effort was so natural it might seem pointless or self-conscious to make something of it. It was what it was. Yet if we stop to consider why it all felt so good, we sense that some deeper process was at work. Expressing our innate generosity, we experienced our "kin"-ship, our "kind"-ness. It was "Us." In service, we taste unity.

~

The state had just released many people from its mental institutions with very little preparation. Our halfway house was about to be flooded with applicants. We had only so much room. Who to shelter? Who to clothe? Who to feed? Deep questions to be faced very suddenly.

An hour before we opened, we agreed to sit together in silence. Meditation, prayer, just plain calming down ... everyone went for their ammo. Then we opened the doors, somehow trusting.

Everything we did, we agreed to do with love. Those people we accepted, we accepted with love. Those we turned away or helped find alternatives ... love. Everyone seemed to understand. The differences between us all, staff and applicants alike, seemed less solid. The whole idea that it all had to do with mental illness even seemed a little artificial. Nobody was really thinking that much, or had time to, or needed to, or something. So much of it was just coming from the heart. So many people, with so many problems. But it went so smoothly. How?

The day after we were done, we sat down to discuss what had happened—your classic evaluation procedure. "Can we come to order?" Which met with some laughter. "So ... ?" someone said. Then this one person stood up and said, "These past three days ... that was about who we all really are. The way we were ... that was the truth about us, deep down."

There was a moment's silence. Someone said, "Right." And that was the meeting. We waited a little longer; you're not used to things becoming clear like that. But after a min-ute or two, people gradually got up and went back to work.

~

Caring for one another, we sometimes glimpse an essential quality of our being. We may be sitting alone, lost in self-doubt or self-pity, when the phone rings with a call from a friend who's *really* depressed. Instinctively, we come out of ourselves, just to be there with her and say a few reassuring words. When we're done, and a little comfort's been shared, we put down the phone and feel a little more at home with ourselves. We're reminded of who we really are and what we have to offer one another.

When the experience of helping seems so natural, it's not surprising we find ourselves wishing or wondering if things could be like that more or even most of the time.

~

I went as a representative of the hippie community of San Francisco to meet the Hopi Indian elders to arrange a Hopi-Hippie Be-In in Grand Canyon. We wanted to honor their tradition and affirm our common respect for the land. As you can guess, this was during the sixties.

Four elders sat at a kitchen table in an adobe building on four chairs. There were no more chairs when I got there. So I sat on the floor kneeling opposite them, so I could see over the table, but under it as well.

The youngest was sixty-five, the eldest one hundred and ten. I could see their hands on their knees under the table. They looked like roots in the earth. There was something so absolutely connected about the whole quality of their pres-ence.

We discussed what it might mean to bring together these different groups and generations of Americans. They told me about difficulties they had been having with white people. One of their braves had recently become involved in an auto accident with a truck from the Bureau of Indian Affairs. The BIA truck had been at fault. But the next day, the BIA found a liquor bottle nearby and claimed the brave had been drinking.

"We called the young man in and we asked him if he had been drinking," one of them told me. He said, "No." And then this elder looked at me very directly and very simply and said, "And he speaks truth."

A chill went through me at that moment. It wasn't just that I believed him or that any doubt or suspicion I might have had was immediately silenced. I experienced a kind of primordial memory of a time when you just spoke truth, a time when relationships were built on trust. That's the way it was done, because that's just how people were.

~

Somewhere deep within many of us is a vision of how helping would flow from trust in ourselves and in others. Or perhaps we might recall images of life in a town in which doors didn't have to be locked, responsibilities were more commonly shared, and going out of your way was hardly out of the ordinary. Or maybe we find ourselves yearning for a future society where the care of others wouldn't have to be mandated. Service wouldn't be a duty, it would be a habit—the way of natural compassion.

And yet . . .

Although at times helping may happen simply in the

way of things, all too often helping isn't happening at all. Even if it is, it can be anything but natural: self-conscious, half-hearted, begrudging. How much are we willing to give, and what are we holding on to? How do we really feel about the place of helping in our lives? We needn't go deep beneath the surface before we encounter our ambivalence. We note the interplay of generosity and resistance, self-sacrifice and self-protectiveness.

What do we hear as we imagine the mind wrestling with the impulses of the heart?

~

Sometimes I help, and sometimes I don't.

I hold the door open for one behind me, or I rush through preoccupied in thought. I vote, but not always. When solicitations come through the mail, some catch my eye or heart and I send at least something. Others I basket as junk mail. A friend is having a hard time. I think I should phone to see how she is, but I just don't feel like doing it tonight.

I'd do anything to help the family. But how much is enough? When to stretch a little further? Whose needs come first?

Those close to me get an immediate hearing. The suffering of people more remote gets sporadic attention. I'm only vaguely aware of it. It's out there somewhere.

Whom should I help anyway? Senior citizens, battered children, human-rights victims, whales? Well, if we don't defuse the nuclear threat, there'll be no tomorrow. But if we don't support education and the arts, what kind of tomorrow will it be?

If I stop to think about it, I help out for all kinds of reasons. Maybe it's because I should; it's a matter of responsi-

bility. But there's usually a maze of other motives: a need for self-esteem, approval, status, power; the desire to feel useful, find intimacy, pay back some debt.

Sometimes I'll help through organizations. But the purpose of helping and the people who really need it often seem to fall through the cracks. Maybe I'd rather do it one-to-one, keep my options open, help out here and there.

I expect my government to relieve suffering. Sometimes it does. But it also pays farmers not to produce wheat while somewhere, every forty-five seconds, a small child starves to death. And a public official, no better or worse a person than I, finds reason to justify this policy—but would probably do everything he could, faced with one starving child.

There are times when service is effortless. Other days, burnout. With one person, I'm totally open and present. With the next, I might as well be on Mars. Sometimes the chance to care for another human being feels like such grace. But later on, I'll hear myself thinking, "Hey, what about me?"

Over Gandhi's tomb are inscribed words that say: Think of the poorest person you have ever seen and ask if your next act will be of any use to him. That'll flash through my mind as I prepare to throw a Frisbee. And when I spend fifteen bucks dining out and going to a movie to ward off boredom, I might recall that a fifteen-dollar operation could restore someone's sight in a third-world country. I'm moved by the power of Gandhi's invitation, "Live simply that others might simply live." But I'm not at all clear about how to heed that, day in and day out, here in the affluent West. Sometimes I feel a little guilty.

I'm fortunate, for the moment, to have good health and loving friends, to be housed and fed, with work to do and some time to play. When I myself need help, there's usually someone to call. I'm able to spend some time away from places where suffering is really visible and just can't be screened out.

Yet there are few days when I'm not feeling human pain, my own or another's. If it's not there in front of me, I see a steady stream of images of misery on the evening news of a suffering planet: homeless one huddled by a doorway or tree; old one looking vacant in a nursing home; slain revolutionary or national guardsman, both teen-agers; drunk driver just realizing he's killed his whole family; starving child's bloated belly and haunted eyes; victims of natural disasters; helpless leaders, helpless helpers.

Some images I ponder; what's that one saying? Others make me uneasy; I tune them out. Some make me angry; I want to get up and do something. Others make me sigh; horror and compassion. And finally I might have to turn away, close off, and escape into some philosophical sanctuary. It's all just too much.

How can I keep my heart open and not go under? I've got my own life to live, after all. Still, I'd like to do more for others. What do I have to offer, and what would help most? Complicated business, all this.

Look, you do the best you can. . . .

~

So we face an interesting situation. Our impulses to care for one another often seem instinctive. The more we're able to act on them freely, the more opportunity we have to feel whole and be helpful. But there are clearly many ways in which we hesitate to reach out or we get confused when we try. The reasons for this don't appear to be simple at all. Perhaps it's due to conditioning or custom.

> *When people lost sight of the way to live*
> *Came codes of love and honesty,*
> *Learning came, charity came,*
> *Hypocrisy took charge;*
> *When differences weakened family ties*
> *Came benevolent fathers and dutiful sons;*
> *Came ministers commended as loyal.*

In *The Way of Life,* written twenty-five hundred years ago, Lao Tsu evokes circumstances that affect us today. We can see them at work even in a very simple request for help. Up comes a stranger and asks, "Can you spare a quarter?" Almost immediately, certain biases rise to the surface and make us hesitate.

Perhaps we hold back because works of compassion have become formalized. We've already put money in the collection plate. We gave at the office. Those funds should have been put to work for this guy already, or they're waiting for him, in one form or another, at the local shelter or soup kitchen. So we're about to say no to his request, but we pause a second longer; we can't quite let it go at that, any more than we can comfortably leave it all to Uncle Sam.

Perhaps we've been taught "family first." Beyond a certain perimeter, our standards change. This fellow asking for money—he's not really "Us." We might feel tentative or hesitant because we haven't had a strong experience of family. As a result of "weakened ties," whether in marriages, between generations, or among distant relatives, our habits of giving have become less than spontaneous. We're not quite sure of what we owe one another even in our immediate circle.

Has our education helped? We've had canned-food drives in school. But have we been brought face to face with those who are hungry? Human need, helplessness, the experience of suffering . . . do we study and discuss these as we grow up?

We probably won't get any sense of who this man asking for money really is, because we find it hard to look him in the eye; we find it hard to look most people in the eye on the street. We stand next to each other in elevators and suddenly get interested in our shoes. In many of our dwellings and communities, we've invested a good deal in our privacy. If we speak infrequently to neighbors, are we any more likely to respond to this stranger? With nothing to go on, we guess who he is. Newly released mental patient? We might go to our pocket. Alcoholic? We'd only be making things worse. Who knows? So we give . . . or we don't . . . and we walk on.

If all these questions and doubts can arise in so ordinary a situation, they'll surely be felt when the demand on us is greater. Do we agree to tithe a portion of our income for famine relief? Do we welcome the establishment of a shelter for the homeless right around the corner? Do we take in our aging father or send him to a nursing home?

The effect of conditioning, of course, doesn't disappear once we've agreed to help out. Whether it's for a few hours a week or as a full-time job, we'll still find ourselves asking where to draw the line, how much we're prepared to give, and what we need to hold on to.

But it's difficult to attribute our uncertainties to the influence of custom and circumstances alone. The roots of these external forces are apparent *within* each of us, if we're the least bit honest with ourselves.

We may cling to familiar circles of association because we're afraid of being rejected. We'll help a friend who understands our sensitivities, but volunteering to cross class lines and work with young unwed mothers might be a little threatening. Are we ready for that? Are they "Us"?

We may have a difficult time facing the suffering of others because we don't know how to deal with *our own* pain and fear. We've waited for weeks to visit a terminally ill colleague with whom we've worked for years. It's clear that it's our own death, not his, we're afraid of, and if we realize that, our guilt may only block us further.

Our choice of how to help may turn on personal motives and needs. We're genuinely eager to aid the physically or mentally ill. But, frankly, we like the status, even the power, of being a "health professional." Some part of us takes pride at being the apparent source of another's well-being.

And when we wonder what we have to offer anyone under any circumstances, aren't we really questioning our self-worth? Whatever outside influences are at work, aren't we still asking the most basic inner question of all: *Who am I?*

Often we reach out to help one another and succeed. The expression of our natural compassion comes easily and we're equal to the challenge. But clearly these deep internal questions of identity and relationship are going to arise much of the time we are caring for one another. The more wrenching the situation, the more likely such issues will be central. Who *are* we to ourselves and to one another?—it will all come down to that.

Will we look within? Can we see that to be of most service to others we must face our own doubts, needs, and resistances? We've never grown without having done so. This wouldn't be the first time we've fought the inertia of conditioning.

Here, then, is a path we can follow in this book, in the company and with the testimony of others like us who are facing these essential questions in their own daily work. We can seek to identify certain basic inner obstacles to the expression of our caring instincts. As these rise to the surface in familiar concrete situations, we can bring them into the clear light of awareness: we see how this resistance is affecting our ability to hear people's needs; how this habit is shaping our attitude to social action; how this expectation is contributing to burnout. By carefully observing these hindrances we can strip away some of their hidden power and reduce their influence over us. With a certain amount of perspective, in fact, we can come to see them not only as problems to overcome but as information leading to a deeper understanding of service. We can make use of them, helping ourselves help others.

As the hold of these obstructions lessens, then, our generosity will flow more spontaneously and effortlessly. Compassion will come forth as needed, as appropriate, simply because it is its nature to do so. Able to help in ways we might not have imagined, we will find this inner work making itself felt in everything we do. Our notion of helping itself will expand. We will grow . . . and be of greater service as a result.

On this path we will stumble, fall, and often look and feel a little foolish. We are confronting long-standing patterns of thought and action. Compassion for ourselves, perspective, humor . . . these are our allies. With their help, we can come to see, in the words of the Bhagavad Gita, that "no step is lost on this path . . . and even a little progress is freedom from fear." The reward, the real grace, of conscious service, then, is the opportunity not only to help relieve suffering but to grow in wisdom, experience greater unity, and have a good time while we're doing it.

~

I'm ninety-two years old, all right. I get up every morning at seven a.m. Each day I remind myself, "Wake up. Get up." I talk to my legs, "Legs, get moving. Legs, you're an antelope." It's a matter of mind over matter. You have to have the right spirit. And I'm out on the streets, seven-thirty a.m. sharp.

I'm wearing my Honorable Sanitation Commissioner badge they gave me from City Hall. I'm alert, I'm ready, I'm out there. And I got my whistle. My job is I help get parked cars off the street so they can bring in the sanitation trucks and the Wayne Broom, the big one—thirty grand for a broom! So when they show up, I go around blowing my whistle to get people to move their cars. I have a great time.

People are asleep. They're busy with businesses. They're busy taking time off from the businesses. They're busy having a good time. They're busy not having a good time.

Whatever. I don't care. I blow my whistle. I'm all over the place.

I don't discriminate, either. I go after the sanitation men too. The union got them a coffee break. Some coffee. They're having eggs, they're having bacon, they're having toast . . . they're having French toast. I kid them about it. And I go right into the restaurant and blow my whistle. They love it, they understand. Everybody loves it, everybody understands. It's the whistle that gets them. Sometimes I'm having such a laugh, I can't blow it. Then I get back to work. "Schleppers, get moving, let's go!"

This used to be a beautiful city. People cared. If you didn't pay your rent, the sheriff would come and put your furniture out on the street. But the poorest of the poor would come automatically and drop their pennies and nickels at your house and put you back into your apartment. That's neighborhood.

Now it's different. Things have gotten out of kilter—hard to say why. People seem to be lost in their own lives. I see them on the street, lost in their own thoughts. Not that I'm all that different. I'm a schlepp myself. I have as many bad habits as anyone. You should see my apartment. It's a mess. Me, Mr. Clean! But I'm trying. Let's try. It's all possible.

What can I tell you? I'm not a saint or a wise man. I'm not the Two-Thousand-Year-Old-Man, I'm only the ninety-two-year-old man. Just a senior citizen. But what do I know that everybody doesn't know? We know. I just go out there in the morning and blow my whistle. That's what I do. You do what you do. Me, I'm having a great time. Wonderful fun. And when people see how much fun I'm having, they have to laugh. What else can they do? Then I hit them with it: "Move your car!"

2
Who's Helping?

In the early stages of my father's cancer, I found it very difficult to know how best to help. I lived a thousand miles away and would come for visits. It was hard seeing him going downhill, harder still feeling so clumsy, not sure what to do, not sure what to say.

Toward the end, I was called to come suddenly. He'd been slipping. I went straight from the airport to the hospital, then directly to the room he was listed in.

When I entered, I saw that I'd made a mistake. There was a very, very old man there, pale and hairless, thin, and breathing with great gasps, fast asleep, seemingly near death. So I turned to find my dad's room. Then I froze. I suddenly realized, "My God, that's him!" I hadn't recognized my own father! It was the single most shocking moment of my life.

Thank God he was asleep. All I could do was sit next to him and try to get past this image before he woke up and saw my shock. I had to look through him and find something beside this astonishing appearance of a father I could barely recognize physically.

By the time he awoke, I'd gotten part of the way. But we were still quite uncomfortable with one another. There was still this sense of distance. We both could feel it. It was very painful. We both were self-conscious . . . infrequent eye contact.

Several days later, I came into his room and found him asleep again. Again such a hard sight. So I sat and looked some more. Suddenly this thought came to me, words of Mother Teresa, describing lepers she cared for as "Christ in all his distressing disguises."

I never had any real relation to Christ at all, and I can't say that I did at that moment. But what came through to me was a feeling for my father's identity as . . . like a child of God. That was who he really was, behind the "distressing disguise." And it was my real identity too, I felt. I felt a great bond with him which wasn't anything like I'd felt as father and daughter.

At that point he woke up and looked at me and said, "Hi." And I looked at him and said, "Hi."

For the remaining months of his life we were totally at peace and comfortable together. No more self-consciousness. No unfinished business. I usually seemed to know just what was needed. I could feed him, shave him, bathe him, hold him up to fix the pillows—all these very intimate things that had been so hard for me earlier.

In a way, this was my father's final gift to me: the chance to see him as something more than my father; the chance to see the common identity of spirit we both shared; the chance to see just how much that makes possible in the way *of love and comfort. And I feel I can call on it now with anyone else.*

~

The most familiar models of who we are—father and daughter, doctor and patient, "helper" and "helped"— often turn out to be major obstacles to the expression of our caring instincts; they limit the full measure of what we have to offer one another. But when we break through and meet in spirit behind our separateness, we experience profound moments of companionship. These, in turn, give us access to deeper and deeper levels of generosity and loving kindness. True compassion arises out of unity.

All the more painful, then, are the moments in which we feel cut off from one another, when we reach out to help or be helped and don't quite meet. Despite the yearning of the heart, so often when we seek to care for one another we feel far apart. Albert Einstein speaks to this question and the challenge it poses to service:

~

A human being is a part of the whole called by us universe, a part limited in time and space. He experiences himself, his thoughts and feelings as something separated from the rest, a kind of optical delusion of his consciousness. This delusion is a kind of prison for us, restricting us to our personal desires and to affection for a few persons nearest to us. Our task must be to free ourselves from this prison by widening our circle of compassion to embrace all living creatures and the whole of nature in its beauty.

Who's Helping?

~

It is to ourselves, then, that we must first look in our effort to see what limits the spontaneous expression of helping instincts. *How does who we think we are affect what we have to give?* How does this "delusion of consciousness" which "separates us from the rest," narrow the range of our compassion? What different understanding of our being might nourish and deepen what we have to offer one another?

All of us seem to be born into the experience of separateness. In infancy, we come to distinguish between "self" and "other." As we develop, we arrive at or devise a complex group of ideas about who we are, our ego. This includes our identity on a variety of planes in which we function simultaneously—as bodies, personalities, citizens, and souls. And we have many roles to play in the course of a single day, each of which is functional and tends to call attention to itself.

Working a busy afternoon at the mental health clinic, we are more conscious of our professional identity. When we get home and see the children, we're most aware of ourselves as parents. Then the evening news comes on, and for a little while we are responding to life, say, as a liberal or as a conservative. The phone rings, and it's our mother; now *we're* someone's child. But that model falls away quickly enough as we prepare for bed, notice that we're aging, wonder about our sex life, and drift off to sleep perhaps anticipating tomorrow's tasks at the clinic.

Hundreds of times a day, we shift costumes to fit appropriate roles. This is the life of the separate self, moving through the world of "other."

For the most part, this model "self" or "ego," with its individual attributes and roles, serves us in good stead. It preserves our physical and, to a degree, our psychological integrity. It gives us a sense of continuity through time, directing and documenting personal growth. It catalogues past experiences, makes available our skills, helps keep track of capacities and limitations.

Frequently we relish or simply enjoy our individuality and sense of uniqueness. The freedom to define who we are is a challenge. As we acquire a certain degree of equanimity in self-image, we are that much more likely to feel empathy for those around us. We know what it's like to be a "self" moving through the world of "others." When someone feels particularly isolated or in pain, we don't need a great deal of information in order to come to his or her aid. Our own experience of separateness guides us to appropriate understanding and support. Perhaps there are more specific parallels of experience. We too have gone through a divorce, lost a loved one, struggled with alcoholism, or experienced a debilitating illness. From this body of common experience, much caring is born. As separate selves, we spend much time reaching out to one another.

Yet it is only fair to say that the quality of our helping sometimes suffers from the hold our sense of separateness might have on us. As happily and healthily as we may function within it, the degree to which we believe ourselves to be individual, isolated entities has consequences for how we care for one another.

Who's Helping?

~

I canvass from door to door looking for voter registration volunteers, asking for just a few hours a week. Not a big job for someone, no great risk, and it can make a difference. That's what we believe, anyway.

What I usually get is a list of reasons Why Not: "I'm busy elsewhere." "I'd be embarrassed to ring someone's door-bell." "What'll I do with the kids?" Things like that.

I'll try to loosen it up a little. "Wouldn't you like to meet some new friends?" "Wouldn't it be nice to not be a mother for three hours a week?"

It generally doesn't break through. And the reasons Why Not usually sound a little hollow as well. Something else is at work.

~

Operating from the model of the separate self, fear and caution may be the first responses we notice that block the spontaneous expression of our innate generosity. In infancy, when the foundation stones of ego are developed and the world seems very big, our survival mechanisms are called into play very quickly. We feel powerless and vulnerable, and because these ideas are learned emotionally, before reason and perspective are fully operating, they may be surprisingly resistant to change as we grow older. So perhaps we are a little wary of the world around us. However much we might wish to reach out, a habit of self-protectiveness buried within may still hold us back. "Keep the doors locked and we'll be secure," says the ego. Our heart responds, "But I'm not happy like that." To which the ego replies, "Better safe than sorry."

We may feel a little nervous and tentative, even defensive, about responding to the needs of others—particularly of those in considerable pain, who may make demands on us, whose reactions may be unpredictable, who may indeed remind us of our own vulnerability. One response of the separate self to the impulse to help out, then, may simply be a reluctance or inability to get involved.

We may also have to contend with inertia. An anxious, self-protective ego is most comfortable in a familiar role in which it knows exactly what's expected of it. This attachment, in the face of changing conditions or new demands, leads the ego to hold on to one model of identity unless it has another equally comfortable one to slip into. It's reluctant to grow, which means opening to the ambiguity of the unknown and learning new roles. This clinging can hold us back from even the simplest actions.

I'm just not the kind of person who signs petitions.

Inasmuch as we are caught up in any sense of personal inadequacy, we may wonder what we really can do for others, even in those moments when we're not fearful or tentative. Because we often identify ourselves, consciously or not, with our shortcomings, we may feel that we don't *have* enough, that we just *aren't* enough, to help meet the needs of others. We give very little because we feel very small.

Who's Helping?

It's not that I don't care—I'm just sure you could find somebody better than me to do it.

Our caution and sense of inadequacy may also lead us to cling to a private agenda that limits the full freedom and generosity of those helpful acts we can initiate. Insofar as we feel lonely, angry, or powerless, for example, our caring efforts may be largely motivated by the need to gain intimacy, vent rage, or win power. Catering to our own needs and expectations, we may be less likely to hear what others feel they really need. We may be willing to give, but our self-image has its terms.

~

Even now, after years of experience, I'm very reluctant to challenge a colleague on a tricky diagnosis. It's a kind of dirty little secret in the medical profession. Everyone has a lot at stake. We all cling to our authority and persona. It becomes a sort of unwritten code among physicians, the license to do that. Very delicate stuff. And who pays, by the way?

~

Frequently, in our efforts to remain secure and protect the integrity of the separate self, we give greater weight to one aspect of our identity over another. Though we may acknowledge, in the abstract, that we are simultaneously physical, emotional, moral, political, and spiritual beings, we seem to cling to one dimension of our identity at the expense of the others. We specialize. As a consequence, however, we often end up shortchanging what we have to offer one another.

"I'm just a surgeon. You really ought to discuss your reactions to this experience with someone else." Why? What of the wellspring of compassion from having seen so many people go through similar experiences as patients? Thinking of ourself simply as a surgeon may cut off access to our empathy, potentially a source of great comfort and counsel.

Or perhaps we think of ourself primarily as a "seeker." "Oh well, I'm basically a religious person. I don't have much to do with politics." Yet by simply opening to acknowledge a fuller sense of identity, we might see that the very inner tranquillity we may have cultivated in spiritual practice is precisely what is needed in social action.

So often we deny ourselves and others the full resources of our being simply because we're in the habit of defining ourselves narrowly and defensively to begin with. Less flexible, less versatile, we inevitably end up being less helpful.

While some self-images are more likely to facilitate the expression of our compassion than others, it is also true that *any* model of the self, positive or negative, will limit our capacity to help. Each form we identify with, each role we attach to, is ultimately incomplete and transient. It can dissolve in a moment. A social worker gets fired— budget cuts, nothing open in the field: "Now I can't even read the want ads." A therapist starts losing patients, and fewer new ones come in: "What's happening? Is it me?" A model mother can't let go as her youngest child turns adolescent: "I'm so depressed. My kids don't need me anymore."

If any of these roles are who we think we are—social worker, therapist, mother—what's left when they fall away? "Where's the rest of me?"

Even if we may momentarily be secure in our chosen roles, they can still impede the quality of our service at the deepest level.

~

I've been chronically ill for twelve years. Stroke. Paralysis. That's what I'm dealing with now. I've gone to rehab program after rehab program. I may be one of the most rehabilitated people on the face of the earth. I should be President.

I've worked with a lot of people, and I've seen many types and attitudes. People try very hard to help me do my best on my own. They understand the importance of that self-sufficiency, and so do I. They're positive and optimistic. I admire them for their perseverance. My body is broken, but they still work very hard with it. They're very dedicated. I have nothing but respect for them.

But I must say this: I have never, ever, met someone who sees me as whole. . . .

Can you understand this? Can you? No one sees me and helps me see myself as being complete, as is. No one really sees how that's true, at the deepest level. Everything else is Band-Aids, you know.

Now I understand that this is what I've got to see for myself, my own wholeness. But when you're talking about what really hurts, and about what I'm really not getting from those who're trying to help me . . . that's it: that feeling of not being seen as whole.

~

Implicit in any model of who *we* think we are is a message to everyone about who *they* are. It's not as if there are any real secrets. If we're only seeing one part of the picture about ourselves, positive or negative, that's all we'll be able to make real to anybody else. Caught in the models of the separate self, then, we end up diminishing one another. The more you think of yourself as a "therapist," the more pressure there is on someone to be a "patient." The more you identify as a "philanthropist," the more compelled someone feels to be a "supplicant." The more you see yourself as a "helper," the more need for people to play the passive "helped." You're buying into, even juicing up, precisely what people who are suffering want to be rid of: limitation, dependency, helplessness, separateness. And that's happening largely as a result of self-image.

To identify with the separate self, however functional it may often be, is to make this model of reality more real for everyone else. How much is this helping, and how much is it hindering?

Perhaps we recognize the predicament; we see the problem of always having to be "somebody." So we decide to let it all go, become the model of humility, and aspire to the ideal of selflessness.

~

One day a rabbi, in a frenzy of religious passion, rushed in before the ark, fell to his knees, and started beating his breast, crying, "I'm nobody! I'm nobody!"

Who's Helping?

The cantor of the synagogue, impressed by this example of spiritual humility, joined the rabbi on his knees. "I'm nobody! I'm nobody!"

The "shamus" (custodian), watching from the corner, couldn't restrain himself, either. He joined the other two on his knees, calling out, "I'm nobody! I'm nobody!"

At which point the rabbi, nudging the cantor with his elbow, pointed at the custodian and said, "Look who thinks he's nobody!"

~

What's to be done? When there's too much "somebody," it's trouble. But we can't make believe we're nobody, either. It's enough to make you throw up your hands and quit!

Time for humor and perspective. The least we can do is acknowledge or remind ourselves that this is part of the predicament of being human. We all must deal with conditioning. The sense of ourselves as separate is what we are contending with virtually all of the time. It's our curriculum, and everybody's enrolled.

So how do we get on with our course of study?

~

As an intern, part of my work was to travel around in teams, examining patients. I would notice their look as we entered. Intimidated, apprehensive, feeling like case studies of various illnesses. I hated that. But I was an intern.

I remember one guy distinctly, however, who was altogether different. I think this guy changed my life. He was a black man in his sixties—very cute, very mischievous, and very sick.

What brought us repeatedly to him was the utter com-

plexity of his illness, condition on top of condition, and the mystery of why he was still alive. It was so strange. We were visiting not to find out what was wrong with him, but why he was still here at all.

I had the feeling he could see right through us. He'd say, "Hey, boys!" when we'd come in—the way you might when a gang of ten-year-olds come barging into a house for a snack in the middle of an intense game outside. He was so pleased, and so amused. It made some people nervous. I was intrigued. But for some weeks, I never had a chance to be alone with him.

Now and then he'd get into very serious trouble, and he'd be moved into intensive care. Then he'd rally, to everyone's amazement, and we'd move him back. And we'd visit him again, and he'd say, "You boys here again?"—pretending to be surprised that *we* were still around.

One night there was an emergency, and I took the initiative and went to see him alone. He looked pretty bad. But he came alert a few seconds after I entered. He gave me a grin and said, "Well . . . ," sort of like he'd expected me. Like he'd known how much I'd come to love him. That happens in hospitals.

I imagine I looked a little surprised at the "Well . . . ," but we just laughed a minute, and I stood there just so taken by who he was. And then he hit me with a single remark, half a question and half a . . . something else.

"Who you?" he said, sort of smiling. Just that. "Who you?"

I started to say, "Well, I'm Doctor. . . ." And then I just stopped cold. It's hard to describe. I just sort of went out. What happened was that all kinds of answers to his ques-

tion started to go through my head. *They all seemed true,
but they all seemed less than true.* "Yeah, I'm this or I'm
that . . . and also . . . but not just . . . and that's not the
whole picture, the whole picture is. . . ." The thought process went something like that. Nothing remotely like that
had ever happened to me. But I remember feeling very
elated.

It must have shown, because he gave me this big grin and
said, "Nice to meet you." His timing killed me.

We talked for five minutes about this and that—nothing
in particular; children, I think. At the end, I ventured to
say, "Is there anything I can do for you?" He said, "No, I'm
just fine. Thanks very much . . . Doctor . . . ?" And he
paused for the name, and I gave it to him this time, and he
grinned at me again, really he did. And that was it.

He died a few days later. And I carry him around today.
I think of him now and again in the midst of my rounds. A
particular moment or particular patient brings him back.
"Who you?" For years, I'd trained to be a physician, and I
almost got lost in it. This man took away my degree, and
then gave it back to me with "And also? . . . and also . . .
and also?" scribbled across. I'll never forget that.

~

How good it can feel to regain perspective. Our feeling of
confinement as narrow, limited, isolated entities begins
to dissolve as we take a few steps back and recognize that
who we are is "this . . . and also . . . and also . . . and
also." Moving in and out of these various identities, each
is "real" only at the moment we are invested in it. A moment later it may not be relevant at all. We see, in other

words, the *relative reality* of these various identities, "real" only in relation to the situation which calls them forth.

But if all of our identities are only relatively real, coming and going as circumstance warrants, is there any part of us that remains steady and stable behind all our roles? If we observe our own minds at work, we see that behind all these identities is a state of awareness that incorporates them all and yet is still able to rest behind them. As we loosen the hold of each identity so that we don't get completely lost in it, we are able to remain light and loose—able to play among these various aspects of being without identifying exclusively with any. We don't have to be anybody in particular. We don't have to be "this" or "that." We are free simply to *be*.

To taste this freedom increases our flexibility immensely, and enables us to be fuller instruments of service to others. For example, as a skillful nurse, we'll sense those moments with certain patients in which all the nurturing we've learned as a mother is needed. Or perhaps a situation arises, say with an imperious physician, when who we are is simply a strong woman—one who's gained that resolve through the consciousness raising and insights of feminism. Or in the presence of one who is dying, we feel that part of ourself which is merely God's child; humility, prayer, and faith are what we have to share now.

We often move among these various identities with much fluidity and skill. When we discover how exhilarating this is, what we're getting is just a taste of real freedom, the liberation that comes from loosening our identification with self-image altogether. We experience the versatility of our being and the independence of our awareness. We're opening up the windows of our little homes and letting in a little cross-ventilation.

Humor also serves to support this awakening perspective. What else, in the end, do we laugh at but our own vanity and puffy attachment to who we think we are? The Marx Brothers have no respect—no respect, that is, for anyone who's busy taking himself seriously as "somebody." Everybody's fair game. Groucho's cracks and Harpo's horn shake us all up. We sit there watching, laughing, loving it, grateful. How often we recognize ourselves in portrayals of human foolishness. How much freer we feel when a friend kids us about some quality of self-importance, and we're able to gulp, take it, and finally join in the general laughter. We come off self-image. We're even able to direct this same irreverence toward our own behavior and attachments.

~

I catch myself in self-importance ten times a day—check that, five—well, maybe once. It's appalling anyway. A little flashbulb goes off and I'm exposed . . . like Jimmy Olsen caught Superman changing clothes in the phone booth.

Of course, whoever I'm with has probably been seeing all this self-importance in me for hours before I ever notice. And my colleagues . . . they've been shrugging or giving up for years. So there's no sanctuary. And I've stopped trying to hide it. No, that's a lie! Don't trust this man! Don't print this interview!

What I've done really is I've begun. I've just started to watch myself as I go through these little prances. I actually have this exercise I sometimes perform. What I do when I catch myself being Mr. Administrator of Social Services is I get up out of my chair, walk away a few steps, stand for a moment, and then turn around and walk back and sit down again. The one who is now seated is usually not the same one who was there before. I'm no longer that guy, Mr. Administrator. For a while, anyway.

I should add that this exercise frequently appears quite mad to other people in the room, particularly if they're people who have come to me for some kind of assistance. ("This is the guy I've come to for help?") Funny. So I perform these exercises at considerable cost to my aura of authority, you understand. But it's definitely worth it. Freedom is priceless . . . worth whatever the cost.

~

With increasing perspective, we see that all of our ego identities, models, and self-images can be useful, but need not be entrapping. We may gain this perspective very slowly, but the direction is clear. As we lighten our attachment to self-image, we find a different vantage point from which to observe who we are.

It's as if you lived in a little town, and you go up to a mountaintop and, looking down, you see how you move about in the course of an ordinary day. You see your route to work, how you go shopping, the main thoroughfares, your shortcuts, your daily routines—you're seeing all that from up there. Then you return to the village. But now, when you're moving around town thereafter, there's a part of you that always recalls the perspective from above. As you go through a day, you're still watching it all from up there.

Sometimes, however, the process of breaking through attachment to our separateness happens simply because we've reached the boundaries of all our roles and self-images: "I gave it everything I had." "I tried everything I knew." Nothing worked, couldn't help. Perhaps we give up in resignation; the separate self, by definition, has its limits, after all. But maybe we find another way. We surrender into the unknown. With nothing left to *do,* we let our heart and intuitive wisdom reveal another way to *be.*

~

You might say I'm the gatekeeper here, the first person people meet when they come in for help. My friends at work, they'll call up and say, "St. Peter?" I say, "He's not here right now, can I take a message?"

Anyhow, Family Services is the name of our department. People come in, I direct them to the appropriate office: food, shelter, child protection, welfare, legal services, your basics. My job is to get a sense of who someone is and then find the right place for them. Not simple.

For a long time I found this an uncomfortable assignment. I don't like sizing up someone according to their problem. It may help them get to the right office, but it also reduces them somehow. Reduces me too. I'll find myself resisting this way of going about things. But I had an experience which changed my way of thinking about it.

There was this woman who was living on the street, one I used to pass on my way to the bus. She was homeless, alcoholic; later it developed she had had a cancer diagnosis. For some reason I decided to take up with her. I liked her smile. Enough of sending everyone elsewhere. I knew the whole maze of social services; I'd take her around myself—clinics, shelters, Medicare, whatever. I guess I wanted to know you could help one person yourself. She was very uncomplaining. Viola. She was willing, even funny about it. "Well, Marie," she'd say, "what are you going to do for me today?"

Oh, the scenes we went through! They called me once from the Women's Shelter. Somehow she'd brought in three pints of Seagram's Seven that night, and a group had gotten drunk. That was against the rules, and I had to take her out. "You told me you'd be good," I said. "You were warm there." She said, "Well, we got warmer."

Or I set her up once with a counselor. After a while he called. "Look, she shows up irregularly, and she always wants to argue with me when she does. What's she here for?" And I'd tell Viola, and she'd say, "Sure, I love to argue with these people. He wants to talk about my childhood all the time. But he doesn't even remember what childhood was like himself. Trust me, Marie."

And I did. I'd have to laugh. She was so insightful and honest. Oh, I really did love her, that one—I really did. But the problems went on for months. Nothing seemed to work out. She kept going back on the street, drinking, getting sicker, all the rest. The more helpless I felt, the more I just loved her; what else could I do? And I'd try again. "Look, Viola," I'd say. "Look where, Marie?" she'd reply. It became a kind of joke between us: "Look." "Look where?"

She moved to a park near my house, and there she started to really go downhill. One evening I went to see her and she was sitting under a tree. She looked awful. I had this powerful feeling that she was getting very close to death. So I went through everything with her one more time: her drinking, her health, her eating, her shelter. *She could come live with me. I'd reached that point of willingness.*

She just listened, and finally she said, "You know, dear, there's nothing you can do for me anymore." And I saw she was right, I just saw that. And I heaved this big sigh, just let go.

About then, it started raining lightly. I finally said, "Well, it's getting late and wet. Shall we go get some coffee?"

She said, "You go, Marie. I'll be all right here."

I said, "Yeah ... well ... I'll see you later then." But somehow it felt to both of us like I wouldn't.

I went to the bus, and I was crying on the bus. I felt just brokenhearted. I felt there was something else, I didn't know what. Then this thought came to me that she was out there alone in the rain. Just that. So I got off and took the other bus back and went into the park with a newspaper on my head. I must have looked pretty funny.

She was under the tree. She looked up at me. I sat down. She said, "What are you doing here?" I said, "Nothing, really. I just felt like being with you a little more." She said, "Okay."

So we sat in the rain. There we were. It was relatively dry, because this was a big sycamore tree. I told her about how my father taught me to identify trees by their bark and how I loved trees and nature and felt happiest there. She told me about the desert. She used to live in Arizona. Her favorite place was the desert; it was so peaceful there.

We watched the rain. We watched how the squirrels ran around and the last few people scurrying out. We watched *how the park looked with no one in it: some birds, a stray dog. . . . some mist beginning to appear. And I felt finally at peace, and we were both at peace, and we stayed silent a long time. I felt such love.*

She walked me to the bus. She said, "Thanks." I said, "For what?" She said, "For nothing." We laughed. "You've been very good to me," she added. We were teary. We hugged. Then I got on the bus, and we waved good-bye. I never saw her again. I'll always love her.

~

When our models of who we are fall away, we are free simply to meet and be together. And when this sense of being encompasses all—one another, the park, the rain, everything—separateness dissolves and we are united in compassion.

Helpful Being, then, is the goal. What we have to offer others will come from our sense of unity. So we look for and cherish those experiences in which we feel ourselves connected to all things in the universe.

Out under the stars, stretching to encompass notions of distance and galaxies, "light years," until the mind just boggles and goes "tilt"—and suddenly your sense of specialness or separateness is replaced by a feeling of identity with the all-inclusive immensity of the universe.

Listening to a Bach chorale and feeling transported into a sense of order and harmony far beyond the music itself.

Harvesting the garden, smiling as you remember the spring planting, and appreciating the lawfulness of fruition in nature, the same life energy in you.

Making love, when you suddenly merge with someone

very dear; two become one, and you somehow feel more truly yourself than you ever had before.

Or in service itself—comforting a crying child, reassuring a frightened patient, bringing a glass of water to a bedridden elder—when you feel yourself to be a vehicle of kindness, an instrument of love. There's more to the deed than the doer and what's been done. You yourself feel transformed and connected to a deeper sense of identity.

~

When I was working in New York with elderly, poor orthodox Jews, I'd come upon a number of old synagogues—dirty, filthy, vandalized. I'd always had ambivalent feelings about synagogues—a kind of no-man's-land for me. If anything, they made me less sure of what it meant to be a Jew.

But one day I came upon one that somehow caught me. That night I went to the service—very few people there, all down and out. And suddenly the thought came to me that I would clean the synagogue. Just that. And I did it.

That's how it began. We'd bring in young people to clean these synagogues and in so doing get a sense of what they really meant—not a social club but a place where the entire life cycle of a people and their continuing relationship with God was to be celebrated.

Myself, I found it hard to pray there. That was the stage I was at. But I helped bring a sense of order and beauty. You see, I had had an immense respect for that generation of Jews which had come to Palestine in the twenties and thirties, who went back to the land not simply to rebuild the land but to be rebuilt by the land, by the work itself.

That's what this became for me. This was a mitzvah, *an*

act of service, but it was also an act by which I myself was being rebuilt— rebuilt into a deeper relationship with my tradition and my people and that living faith.

~

Finally, profound moments of spiritual and religious experience take us beyond identification with our isolated egos. The sense of separateness falls away as we come into some deeper understanding of "It All." While these experiences do not always easily lend themselves to words, the message of all the teachings that support them have much in common. Don't get lost in what's apparent. Go beyond the evidence of the senses and the rational mind. Acknowledge that there are more things in heaven and earth than are dreamt of in our philosophies. Whatever else we may seem to be, we're also reflections or expressions of ... and then we get names for the nameless: "Awareness," "Being," "God," "Life," "the Formless," "the Way." Whatever it is, whatever it's called, *there's only One of it.* It's present in all creation. We ourselves are rooted in it. It is our essence.

Who we are, from this perspective, *begins with the One.* Unity, not separateness, is our starting point. And while our ego doesn't disappear, its importance is certainly put in perspective as a result of having experienced a higher Self.

Whether these experiences—through nature, art, love, service, spirit—are frequent or rare, we see that when we are not caught up in self-conscious separateness, not defined by self-image, we still survive. Indeed, we thrive and function happily, freely, and efficiently. We feel ex-

alted. Despite all our ego's concerns and warnings of the
dire consequences of not being "somebody special," we
are capable of simply resting in our being. We simply *are*.

> *The geese have no intention to cast their reflections.*
> *The lake has no mind to receive their image.*
>
> Fortune Cookie

From this perspective, the whole question of identity can
look very different. We can enter into the world of the
separate self with a certain amount of freedom, even
irony and whimsy. As long as we're here, we might as
well play.

~

In a Seattle newspaper there was a picture of a man behind
bars. The caption explained that he had been caught with a
dispatch case full of papers and cards claiming various and
different identities. The police had thus far ascertained that
he was none of these. The problem was that they couldn't
find out who he really was.

The man said, "They're the ones who arrested me. It's
their problem to find out who I am. I know who I am." The
police sergeant said, "This man has boggled our system."

~

Tastes of self-transcendence draw us to further exploration. We recognize that these insights need to be cultivated. We may easily fall back into old habits and
patterns of thought. But having come into contact with
the higher Self, we're motivated to find ways to

strengthen our acquaintance. There are many paths, and each in its own way can help us to move beyond identification with the separate isolated ego.

To study the Way is to study the Self.
To study the Self is to forget the Self.
To forget the Self is to be enlightened by all things.
To be enlightened by all things is to remove the barrier between Self and Other.

DOGEN ZENJI

We may choose to explore those forms of therapy that encourage us to understand just how our models of self have arisen through past experience. Earlier forms of psychotherapy seemed to deify the ego and, by focusing on its genesis, invest it with more and more solid reality. Recent approaches of transpersonal, humanistic, and Gestalt therapies, and those derived from Jung, encourage the liberation of the self and the exploration of a more expansive sense of identity.

As we shall see in a subsequent chapter, the practice of meditation can help us to develop our ability to penetrate the process whereby the mind is constantly creating and reinforcing attributes of the separate self, ideas of "me." We can systematically observe these ideas as they pass by, seeking to draw us into identification: "I'm this, I'm that." But we can learn to remain mindful behind these thoughts, lessening our attachment to them as we watch them rise and pass away.

Other traditions, in effect, use the mind to beat the mind. In Rinzai Zen Buddhism, a teacher gives a student a particular koan to solve—for example, "What was your original face before you were born?" Of course, no rational answer is possible. But the student makes regular appearances to offer a response. Usually he comes armed with some artifice designed to make him appear wise and insightful. But these answers are quickly discerned as creations of ego and brusquely dismissed, and the student is rejected. This continues until the moment the student gives up the effort to look impressive and a spontaneous answer just comes out. The teacher honors it. The student has "forgotten the self."

Some of us may experience the call to congregation and find ourselves drawn deeply to collective devotion and ritual. Whether in worship, formal ceremony, song, dance, or services, we experience the coming together of our many hearts. As joy and exaltation grow, our sense of separateness falls away. This becomes our path for strengthening our sense of unity.

Or perhaps the experience comes through solitary, interior prayer and contemplation. We lift up our hearts, minds, and souls. We reach out to God. Through our surrender, love, and faith, we feel a sense of profound communion in which our individuality merges into His Being. In these moments we are One. And though they may not last or retain their intensity, we're not likely to forget these moments when they happen. We seek them more often.

All these methods, and many others, strengthen our ability to recognize and dwell in our higher Self, beyond separateness. In pursuing these practices, however, it's important to remember that the object is not to destroy the ego. We're not declaring war on our separate self. It helps assure our survival and effectiveness. It has a role to play at an appropriate level of our lives. What we're doing instead is working to establish a new balance between the ego and the higher Self and allowing our higher Self to expand, explore, and root itself more fully in a consciousness of unity.

Ramakrishna, the great Indian saint, likened the situation to a coach in which the driver (the ego) sits atop in command of the horses. The owner (the higher Self) sits quietly within. Because the coachman has never seen the owner, he begins to think himself totally in charge. But when the owner makes himself known, quietly but firmly, the coachman, perhaps begrudgingly but ultimately in his best interests, relinquishes his fantasy and becomes content in the role of . . . of what? Of *servant,* it turns out. For then it responds more and more to the call "Not my but Thy Will, O Lord." The ego finds joy and relief in attuning to the greater Way of All Things, to the larger harmonies of the universe in which it can find its proper place and need no longer be driven by the insatiable need to control. In surrender to its proper station, the ego finds peace. The higher Self is now freer to guide the work of loving kindness and compassion. The character of service also.begins to change.

~

Now there are two theories about crime and how to deal with it. Anticrime guys say, "You have to think like a criminal." And some police learn that so well they get a kind of criminal mentality themselves.

How I'm working with it is really pretty different. I see that man is essentially pure and innocent and of one good nature. That's who he is by birthright. And that's what I'm

affirming in the course of a day on the job. In fact, *that is my
job*. The "cop" part of it . . . well, they call us "cops"; to me,
my job is I'm a peace officer.

Now it's interesting how this works. For example, when
you are holding in thought a vision of our unity in good,
you frequently spot a criminal motive arising or evident in
someone. It's a kind of spiritual radar. Crimes can be prevented that way—I've seen that. And not only that. At the
same time, I'm holding to the view that such a person is
complete already, and doesn't need to steal, and will be
provided for from universal abundance. So I work not only
to prevent the crime but to eliminate its causes—its causes
in fear and greed, not just the social causes everyone talks
about.

Even when it gets to conflict. I had arrested a very angry
black man who singled me out for real animosity. When I
had to take him to a paddy wagon, he spit in my face—that
was something—and he went after me with a chair. We
handcuffed him and put him in the truck. Well, on the way,
I just had to get past this picture of things, and again I af-
firmed to myself, "This guy and I are brothers in love."
When I got to the station, I was moved spontaneously to
say, "Look, if I've done anything to offend you, I apologize." The paddy wagon driver looked at me as if I was totally nuts.

The next day I had to take him from where he'd been
housed overnight to criminal court. When I picked him up,
I thought, "Well, if you trust this vision, you're not going to
have to handcuff him." And I didn't. We got to a spot in
the middle of the corridor which was the place where he'd
have jumped me if he had that intention. And he stopped
suddenly. So did I. Then he said, "You know, I thought

*about what you said yesterday, and I want to apologize." I
just felt this deep appreciation.*

*Turned out on his rap sheet he'd done a lot of time in
Michigan and had trouble with guards in jail. I symbolized
something. And I saw that turn around, saw a kind of healing, I believe.*

*So what really happens if you're going to explore
whether or not this vision of our nature really has power?
Maybe people will say you're taking chances. But you're
taking chances without any vision; your vision is your protection. Maybe they'll say you're sentimentalizing people.
But it's not about people. It's about principle and truth. It's
about how the universe is. Maybe they'll think it's idealis-
tic; things could never be this way. Well, for me, things are
this way already; it's just up to us to know that more clearly.*

*I see that my work is to hold to an image of who we all
truly are, and to be guided by that. And I have been guided
by that. To greater strength and security . . . within myself
and on the street.*

~

What follows in the quality of our helping when we
begin to know ourselves beyond separateness?

Perhaps, at the very least, we can be a little less fearful,
a little more trusting. When we break through the
boundaries of self, we often find that we don't have to be
as defensive as we might have thought or as might have
been our habit. Things aren't inevitably pitted against
us. If they appear to be, the possibility of harmony and
reconciliation is a little more real. When we've had a
taste of unity, we're that much more ready to bring it

quickly into any situation, at any given moment, with anybody.

We'll also be more likely to take initiative and to reach out less self-consciously to those in need. Someone may be a little shy asking for help, and we ourselves may be a little tentative offering it. But we can overcome these boundaries more quickly because we've already been working to see that they're not inevitably so solid. How many times, after all, do we initially hold back with one another, only to laugh when we finally break through the caution and meet openly and freely? How long it takes for this to happen depends entirely upon how much we're coming into these situations feeling separate. What's to prevent us from meeting in compassion instantaneously?

The more we're able to take such initiative trustingly, the greater sense of range and possibility we're likely to have in our efforts to help out. We might feel more patience—we'll work longer and harder with a retarded child or someone in physical therapy—when we have more confidence that there are sources of support beyond ourselves. Something may happen, someone may come along, a moment of insight, a flash of inspiration, a new source of energy. We're more trusting of the universe because we have experienced nourishment in those moments when we've felt at One with it.

Being less cautious, we'll be more likely to take risks in the expression of our helping instincts. Perhaps in the midst of a grim situation near a family sickbed, heads shaking, brows all furrowed, we'll take a chance and say, "This is quite a soap opera we're all stuck in here." Now maybe they'll throw us right out of the room; *that's* how much of a soap opera it is. But maybe it'll be just what's needed to break the tension. Maybe a few people will be able to come up for a moment's air, see the horizon beyond the next wave, remember the big picture, then take a deep breath before plunging back in the midst of it all. We've succeeded in interrupting the soap opera for a brief public service message. Worth a try anyhow. At the very least, we're seeing that we can stretch ourselves, go beyond what's familiar, trust our instincts a little more. All this is possible because we're not so firmly wed to models of ourselves and how we're supposed to behave when we're seeking to help one another. Less afraid that reaching out threatens our own well-being, we're freer and more venturesome in expressing our caring instincts.

As we approach other people in this spirit, we'll also be more likely to communicate what we have in common rather than what divides us. Knocking on someone's door with a petition protesting utility rates, we won't have to meet as "righteous activist" and "reluctant housewife." Maybe we'll get engrossed in the smell of the soup inside as the door opens. We'll begin talking recipes, talking grandparents' recipes, talking grandparents . . . and then, almost as an afterthought, "Oh, by the way, I had this petition. I don't know about *your* utility rates, but ours . . ." "Oh, yes. Ours too. I don't usually get involved in this stuff, but sure, right—where do I sign?"

As we become less identified with any single aspect of the separate self against another, we're freer to know which among them all is most appropriate for a given situation. It's as if we can be anyone to anyone. Resting behind all roles, we can also be, as it were, no one to no one—that is, we can create a space where whoever we're with has the best chance to come out from behind *their* self-image. No costumes, no disguises; come as you are.

The awareness that allows us to rest behind ego, moreover, also gives us a far greater ability to listen to others, to hear what's really needed. Our intuition can guide our actions. The universe is filled with information. Answers are inherent in questions. The less our mind is busy feeding the ego, the more we can allow our "spiritual radar" to come into play, the more we can tune into One Mind.

Our work to move beyond separateness may also strengthen our sense of abundance. We feel like we need less because we're coming to see just how much we'll always have access to. We don't have to ration our helping acts quite so carefully. We needn't constantly measure just how much we'll be able to offer before we get depleted. We don't have to feel as if we are sacrificing by giving. Beyond separateness, service replenishes. "To forget the Self is to be enlightened by all things."

In turn, our helping actions will be less directed by the ego's personal agenda and need for constant reassurance. We won't be entering into service so much to gain intimacy, purpose, a sense of usefulness, and so on. We don't need to go anywhere special to attain these. They're in us already and available all around, simply as we understand our interrelatedness with all things. Our service, then, is less a function of personal motive and more an expression of spontaneous, appropriate caring.

We're not so much helping out, then, because it's "me" needing to tend to "you." We're helping out because it's "*Us.*" The more we understand and dwell in that truth, the more we serve simply in the way of things. If one of "Us" needs help, if one of Our arms gets caught in a door, naturally we use the other of Our arms to set it free. Helping happens not because it's been weighed and considered; it happens because the barriers to its lawful and automatic expression have fallen away.

And, finally, what of those moments when we question whether we've anything useful for others? What do we really have to offer, what do we really have to give? *Everything,* it turns out. Everything. If within each of us is that essence of Being which is in all things—call it God, Life, Energy, Consciousness—as open to all that as we are in ourselves, so we have it to share with one another.

What could that mean practically, as more than a lofty abstraction? It could mean that when we're holding a frightened, battered child . . . or hearing the grief of a total stranger . . . or bandaging the wound of an enemy soldier . . . or sitting with a dying friend . . . they can feel in *who we are* the reassurance that they are not simply isolated entities, separate selves, lonely beings, cut off from everything and everyone else. They can feel us *in there* with them. They can feel the comfort that we are all of us in this together. They have the chance to know, in moments of great pain, that nevertheless we are Not Separate.

When all else fails, when we've done what we can, we still have this essential reassurance to offer one another. It comes as each of us moves beyond attachment to separateness into a greater sense of Unity. "To be enlightened by all things is to remove the barrier between Self and Other."

3
Suffering

M*y idea was pretty simple at the beginning. I started to volunteer in wards with terminally ill children or burn victims—just go in there to cheer them up a little, spread around some giggles. Gradually, it developed that I was going to come in as a clown.*

First, somebody gave me a red rubber nose, and I put that to work. Then I started doing some elementary makeup. Then I got a yellow, red, and green clown suit. Finally, some nifty, tremendous wing-tip shoes, about two and a half feet long, with green tips and heels, white in the middle. They came from a clown who was retiring and wanted his feet to keep on walking.

It's a little tricky coming in. Some kids, when they see a clown, they think they're going to be eaten alive. And kids in hospitals and burn units, of course, are pretty shaky. So it's always good to lead with some bubbles, just blow some bubbles around the ward. Then I'll move from bed to bed, just feeling out what's appropriate: maybe checkers, or blackjack, or go-fish. Or if they're lying there with tubes coming out of them, I'll hit the kids with riddles. Riddles are great.

Later, if they can manage it, I'll give them this paper bag that they can fit over their heads. When they put it on and sort of blow their lips together, they can make this crazy sound I call the Funny Mantra. They turn into a living kazoo. I'll say, "If things get too tough, just take that paper bag from under your pillow and sound off. Maybe that'll help a little, and it'll sure surprise the nurses."

Because things do get very tough in there, I'll tell you. They were very tough for me at the beginning—very. You see some pretty terrible things in these wards. Seeing children dying or mutilated is nothing most of us ever get prepared for. Nobody teaches us to face suffering in this society. We never talk about it until we get hit in the face.

Like when I was starting out I was making the rounds one day at a children's hospital. The shade was pulled on this one room so I couldn't see, but I peeked in the door. It was a room with badly burned children in it. They had them in chrome crib beds with walls on the side, so they couldn't crawl out or fall out if it got too terrible in there.

There was this one little black kid in one of them. He was horribly burned. He looked like burnt toast. Pieces of his face weren't there. Pieces of his ears were missing. Where was his mouth? You could hardly tell who he was. There was no way of pinning a person to the face, what little there was of it.

It was just terrible, just mind-boggling. My jaw dropped, I gasped, and I came completely unglued. I remember flashing back to the antiwar movement. There was a picture of a napalmed kid I used to carry around at demonstrations. Suddenly here was that kid right in front of me. Unbelievably painful to behold.

I was overwhelmed. And my mind went off in all sorts of directions. "What's it going to be like if he lives?" "What if I had a child this happened to?" "What if this happened to me?"

So there we were, burnt toast and unglued clown. Quite a sight, I bet. And I'm fighting just to stay there, trying to find a way to get past my horror.

All of a sudden, this other little kid comes whizzing by—I think he was skating along with his IV pole—and he stops, and kinda pushes around me, and looks into the crib at this other kid, and comes out with, "Hey. YOU UGLY!" Just like that. And the burnt kid made this gurgling laugh kind of noise and his face moved around, and all of a sudden I just went for his eyes, and we locked up right there, and everything else just dissolved. It was like going through a tunnel right to his heart. And all the burnt flesh disappeared, and I saw him from another place. We settled right in.

"YOU UGLY!" Right. He ugly. He probably knows how ugly he is more than anyone else. And if he's gotta deal with people hanging around with saliva coming out of their mouths, it's gonna be extra horrible. But if somebody just meets him in the eye and says, "Hey, what's happening? Wanna hear a riddle. . . ?"

So being able to look You Ugly in the eye . . . that's done a lot for me. Because once I do that, I can go on to see what might be done that can ease things up. And you get all kinds of inspiration.

Like, some of us were setting up to show *Godzilla* in the

kids' leukemia ward. I was making up kids as clowns. One kid was totally bald from chemotherapy, and when I finished doing his face, another kid said, "Go on and do the rest of his head." The kid loved the idea. And when I was done, his sister said, "Hey, we can show the movie on Billy's head." And he really loved that idea. So we set up Godzilla and ran it on Billy's head, and Billy was pleased as punch, and we were all mighty proud of Billy. It was quite a moment. Especially when the doctors arrived.

So I don't know. Burnt skin or bald heads on little kids— what do you do? I guess you just face it—when the kids are really hurting so bad, and so afraid, and probably dying, and everybody's heart is breaking. Face it, and see what happens after that, see what to do next.

I got the idea of traveling with popcorn. When a kid is crying I dab up the tears with the popcorn and pop it into my mouth or into his or hers. We sit around together and eat the tears.

~

Suffering seems to be a fact of life. How do we face it? Clearly it is a stranger to none of us. Perhaps we've not experienced the corrosive pain of illness, persecution, starvation, or violence. We may not have lived with the deterioration and loss of a loved one. Few of us have seen the charred face of a burned child. But each of us has experienced our fair share of not getting what we want or having to deal with what we don't want. In this, we all know suffering.

The way in which we deal with suffering has much to do with the way in which we are able to be of service to others. Of course, not all helping revolves around suffering. Much of what we offer may be in the nature of simple support or guidance: moving a friend's new furniture, teaching a child to read. But it is the affliction of others that most directly awakens in us the desire to be of care and comfort.

The impulse to do all we can to relieve one another's pain is the automatic response of our native compassion. But the experience of suffering—in ourselves and in others—triggers off complicated reactions. To investigate these is itself an act of compassion, an essential step toward becoming more effective instruments of mutual support and healing. How then do we respond to the pain we see around us? And, once we have investigated this response, how do we respond to our own afflictions?

At one level, we seem to have an attraction-aversion relationship to human suffering. Sometimes our attraction seems to take a neurotic form. It seems to trigger off an almost morbid fascination. We continually feed ourselves, through newspapers, soap operas, tragedies, and gossip with images of suffering. It's as if our vicarious involvement with the trials and tribulations of others engages us in the life process in a way that we seem to need but also want to be able to control. We want to watch it, but be able to turn it off at will.

At another and deeper level, however, the suffering of others spontaneously awakens a response of instant empathy.

You're right behind a man on the unemployment line. His eyes are red: you can tell he's been drinking. He finally gets his turn after waiting three hours, only to be told he's got to come back with the right papers. He's confused, but he nods; he doesn't want to make trouble. But as he leaves the line, you can tell he didn't get it quite right, and he probably won't make it back next week. He's heading for a bar and it's ten-thirty in the morning.

Your closest friends, married for twenty years, are fighting bitterly, right there in the restaurant, right there in front of you and their kids. You've never seen them act that way before. The marriage is falling apart. One daughter is staring at her soup. The other flashes you a look of panic.

Your heart goes out to them, goes out to them all. The pain of others gives rise to a desire to help, to comfort, to touch, to say "I'm here, I'm with you, I understand."

But it's one thing to have one's heart engaged, quite another to have it overwhelmed or broken. Here lies our aversion to suffering. For when it gets too close and too strong—the terrible suffering of a parent, child, lover, best friend—we may experience a pain so excruciating that it can threaten the very fabric of our being, shatter our tenuously held faith, and cast us into deepest despair.

Between the event to which we feel no personal connection and a tragedy that breaks our hearts, there is a vast range of affliction. In this domain we make our choices: Shall I become involved or not, and if so, how deeply? How much human pain to let in, and whose? Because the suffering around us is endless, the choices before us seem limitless. We must weigh them carefully, lest, once we have opened Pandora's box, pain overwhelm us, and jeopardize our fragile control of the universe around.

This *range* of choices is recent and perhaps unique to our present culture. Where people live their whole lives in close proximity, there's very little choice. Suffering involves all. The village's orphans are everybody's children.

But affluence has bought us privacy, and the apparent power to guard it against the encroachments of other people's adversity. As individuals and as a society, we set up lines of defense. We isolate poverty, old age, and death so that we need not confront them in our daily lives. The poor are off in ghettos, the elderly in retirement homes, the dying in terminal care wards. We pay to push suffering away.

But privacy exacts its costs. How quickly, for example, it turns to loneliness and alienation. Our defense against one kind of suffering, ironically, turns out to have invited in another. We may somehow feel safe from the troubles of the world, but we also begin to feel dry, empty, and alone in our insulated havens. Gone is the mutuality and spontaneous support that arise naturally when lives are led in common. With doors closed to the pain of others, we banish that which would release our compassion and engagement with life. We need heart-to-heart resuscitation.

Nor does the privacy actually end up buying us any final protection. Despite it, we're still interconnected with the peoples of the planet. While our isolation may give us some degree of temporary peace, there's little security in peace based on exclusion. As America has found out, the insistent goad of the world's suffering will ultimately force entry even into our well-protected castle. The pain and anger of those who are oppressed shape the challenges of our political life. If their suffering seems abstract, it is nonetheless ever present through networks of communication which extend our knowledge of human affliction to the outermost reaches of the planet. We can push it all away only so far.

Because our privacy is finally unfulfilling, and the pain of others ultimately can't be ignored, we find we must choose how much suffering we can let in, and what to do with it once it's there.

These choices are usually made in the midst of a mighty struggle between the head and the heart.

The suffering of others spontaneously releases our desire to help out. Our heart begins to open. But then there's a thought: Is this problem too heavy? Do I have what it takes? If I offer to help, will I ever get away? Set off by fear, the mind is startled into self-defense. The fear, of course, is in part a reaction to the suffering itself. But it is also a response of resistance to the heart's natural compassion as it reaches out to engage someone's pain.

Fear is the mind's reaction against the inherent generosity of the heart. Because the heart knows no bounds to its giving, the mind feels called upon to define limits. Under such tension, little wonder our choices of how to respond to the pain of others seem so difficult.

Perhaps we seek to resolve this tension without really having to open the door to suffering: a quick call to a sick friend; a charitable contribution slipped through the mail slot; some grain to a third-world country. But do these measures really feed and satisfy the heart, our own and others'? As useful as they may be, they often short-change our compassion. We know there's more to help-ing than this.

Perhaps we open the door partway. We define bound-aries of time and space for our involvement: a year off for the Peace Corps; every Tuesday morning at the battered women's shelter; eight hours a week with AIDS patients. We'll vote ourselves, but we won't go out to register others. "I'll visit Aunt Rosie in the convalescent home, but I won't bring her back to my house." Our service takes place in the fifty-minute hour. Careful boundaries assure that suffering won't spill over into the rest of our lives. These may be necessary; we all have other commit-ments. As often as not, however, they are artificially con-trived to ward off that loss of control which so threatens and frightens the mind.

But frequently these gestures fall short. Our bound-aries prove to be Maginot Lines. Suffering presses through. So we retreat to our next line of defense: the mind itself and its array of tactics to protect its security in the face of pain.

There is, for example, the early-warning system of de-nial which often comes into play almost automatically. We blot out the suffering right before our eyes. We walk down the street past beggars and people obviously in pain without even noticing them. An ambulance goes by; it's just a loud noise, it'll pass. We hear cries in the night; it's only a family feud, we turn over and go back to sleep. Potential nuclear annihilation is only twenty minutes away; we can't handle the thought of it. It's as if we have an invisible screen that deflects evidence of pain as soon as it gets close enough. How easily we delete it from awareness, without even being aware that we've done so.

> About suffering they were never wrong,
> The Old Masters: how well they
>   understood
> Its human position; how it takes place
> While someone else is eating or opening a
>   window or just walking dully along.
>
> W. H. AUDEN

When this early-warning system fails, the mind must call on other devices in its repertory of response to suffering and the fear of it. One tactic is so simple we usually fail to notice it. We put some concept or idea between ourselves and the suffering. In comes Mary Jones, hurting real bad. As she sits across the desk she suddenly becomes Mary Jones, "schizophrenic." With a flick of the mind, we've turned a person into a problem.

Or we try to stuff suffering into a facile spiritual or philosophical perspective: "It's just the way of things." "Suffering is part of the Grand Plan." "It's their karma." "Suffering is grace." A party line, glib and heartless.

Sometimes we even use the fact of human suffering to justify abstract ideologies. We use it to prove points.

~

I broke with a certain circle of antiwar friends, best friends, when dead lives became souvenirs.

Some young Americans were invited to Czechoslovakia to meet the representative of the Viet Cong, the NLF. At the end they were given rings of friendship. They were made of steel from shot-down American planes.

Now maybe to some that meant swords into plowshares. But for most, those rings were status symbols, radical macho. They got passed out very selectively. I didn't hear any talk about the pilots of those planes and their families.

It sounds extreme. But the same thing happened with the slaughter at My Lai and television images of our soldiers burning village huts. Some people were more glad to see those images than they were pained by the death of innocent civilians. You could really see that. Antiwar people, all these.

~

"The greatest sin of the age," wrote the Russian philosopher Nicholas Berdyaev, "is to make the concrete abstract." That's what the mind is trying to do through all these devices, and through efforts to explain things away. (Someone falls, and our attention turns quickly from the person to the slippery streets: "They really should do something about that.") Frequently these devices have the stink of self-righteousness about them—banishing the suffering from our awareness and making us feel good about ourselves at the same time. "If she wasn't a drunkard, she wouldn't have ended up that way." "Well, they always cut school, no wonder they can't find a job." "If those people in India didn't spend so much time meditating, they'd have their economic scene together and there wouldn't be so much starvation."

Pity is another way we keep suffering at arm's length. We may let in a little of someone's pain, but never enough to threaten our own self-control. We may feel a little moved to respond to the suffering—we'd feel guilty or uncomfortable if we didn't—but we'd like to get it all over with as soon as possible and get on with our own affairs. Compassion and pity are very different. Whereas compassion reflects the yearning of the heart to merge and take on some of the suffering, pity is a controlled set of thoughts designed to assure separateness. Compassion is the spontaneous response of love; pity, the involuntary reflex of fear.

~

When you're blind, you hear very well. The tone of someone's voice is their face. It never lies. And I'll hear the difference between someone just caring for me and someone protecting themselves. Like, they want to be concerned. They don't want to get up and leave. But their mind is elsewhere. And what I hear is their fear and guilt—even in the middle of their concern. It's such a mixed signal.

~

Perhaps the strategy for dealing with suffering most familiar in our helping institutions is that of "professional warmth." Like pity, it's a stance to keep our distance. Since many professionals even believe that it's appropriate "not to get involved," they demonstrate a cool efficiency and impersonal friendliness, at best a façade, at worst plain hypocrisy. They become like their machines: cool green, giving off a competent hum. It's a way of plasticizing human relationships to keep them sterile, free of contact germs.

Of course it's understandable how this state of affairs

has evolved. The demands on helping professionals to confront so much suffering each day are immense. "Professional warmth" is a survival strategy. But it's no answer. Our hearts pay the price, helpers and helped alike. Fortunately, awareness of this problem is growing. "The question of suffering and its relation to organic illness has rarely been addressed in the medical literature," reported the prestigious *New England Journal of Medicine* in a special article devoted to this issue. But what does it say about our habits that this concern has been such a long time coming?

Frequently, our reactiveness to suffering takes the form of having instantly to do something, do anything. It's the "we gotta" syndrome: "We gotta" fix this up right away. "We gotta" call this person for advice. It's tricky, because this impulse may arise from genuine empathy, but the form of action is compulsive. Often what's happening is that "we gotta" get rid of someone's pain because it's hurting *us* too much. Its true neurotic dimension is most evident when there's really nothing to do, yet still we must talk to that nurse, question that doctor, call that specialist, rearrange the furniture, change the TV channel, straighten the bed (for the fifth time in the last twenty minutes)—and "Are you sure you're all right, dear? Really? I mean, really?"

Rushing about with this reactive and zealous urgency infects the situation with a toxic tension which is the last kind of mental state anyone who's suffering needs. This agitation perpetuates itself and compounds suffering. It's Typhoid Mary disguised as Florence Nightingale. In a helpless lay person, such behavior can be flamboyant. In a helping professional, it's often more subtle.

How Can I Help?

Denial, abstraction, pity, professional warmth, compulsive hyperactivity: these are a few of the ways in which the mind reacts to suffering and attempts to restrict or direct the natural compassion of the heart. This tension between head and heart leaves us tentative and confused. As we reach out, then pull back, love and fear are pitted against one another. As hard as this is for *us*, what must it be like for those who need our help?

~

Being a long-term patient gives you a unique perspective on the world, and I have to laugh, although sometimes I must say it's a little bittersweet.

Naturally, I'm seen as helpless. They have to lift me, move me, deal with my bowels and all. I don't look very nice or smell very nice, I suppose. What I often see coming in the room is what you might call Central Casting for "General Hospital."

Here comes Miss Aren't-You-Looking-Better-Today. Which is funny to me, since it's pretty clear I'm only barely holding my own. Enter stage left we have Nurse Wince. It's hard for her to look at me. She's afraid for her own mother, that she'll end up like me. The doctors stride in; they should play "Pomp and Circumstance" over the PA system regularly. They're examining my case. They find my case interesting. My visitors . . . they usually fall into the soap opera too. And so do I, I suppose.

On it goes. You'd be surprised at the number of people who talk to you and can't look you in the eye, even more than we normally can't look each other in the eye. It's like a parade of attitudes in here.

It's funny; I laugh. I understand, I really do. I'm not a

*pretty picture. Their work is hard. But sometimes I just
want to cry out, "Hello! Is anybody there? Hello? Hello?"*

~

How can we answer back . . . and in a way that our answers are heard and welcomed? How, in other words, can
we engage suffering and stay open to the expression of
our natural compassion?

First, perhaps, we can start out by just asking these
questions of ourselves. They frame the situation in such a
way that we can once again open ourselves to new possibilities of response to suffering. They can turn our attention to an examination of the reactions that suffering
triggers off in us. Up to now these reactions have been
rooted not only in fear but in the *denial* of fear. Merely to
be mindful of this pattern is to be one step closer to our
own truth and, in turn, to the truth of someone else's suffering. *Truth* is where we will meet. Simply acknowledging our reactiveness to pain, therefore, is itself an initial
act of service.

~

*As I walk into the sanatorium, I have a little exercise. I
know that I'm to be presented with evidence of terrible
pain. It's all right there, right in front of me. And I know
that it's probably going to blow me away the minute I go
in, no matter that I've worked there six years. So I'll take
note of all that, as if it were a sign on the front door. It gives
me a certain amount of sobriety—preparation for entering.*

*In doing that, I find I get a feeling of deep respect for
those inside who are suffering from the kinds of pains
they're dealing with. Basic respect for their dignity and*

their worth. They're here, they're equally as human as I am, and their suffering calls my attention to that fact.

Sometimes I also find myself honoring them. Not just respect, but honoring them for what they are and what they're enduring. I'll try to bring that feeling in the door with me. This gives me strength. And it just starts simply from taking account of what's going on in me, in the sanatorium, in those inside it.

~

Our tendency when we acknowledge qualities in ourselves like fear of suffering or loss of control may be to judge ourselves. Found selfish, uncaring, impatient, unworthy . . . we're embarrassed and uncomfortable at the recognition of our "weakness." We have not taken to heart the example of the biblical Paul, who said, "My strength is made perfect through weakness." Yet this often turns out to be the case in our efforts to care for others. Acknowledging our weakness can soften our defensiveness. We're not so busy protecting ourselves all the time. We're much more likely to be there for anyone who is wrestling with his or her own sense of weakness, unworthiness, or fear. We'll hear each other. To acknowledge our humanness, with its mixture of empathy and fear, strengthens our helping hand.

But we must do so with compassion for ourselves and a supportive appreciation of our own predicament. Such compassion can come forth more easily when we appreciate that *it is the openness of our heart, after all, with which this all began.* Our fear is awakened not just by the suffering but by the intensity of our heart's reaction to it. The ego may have been frightened into all kinds of defense mechanisms to control our innate generosity. But mercy and kindness were our first impulses. Natural compassion was our starting point.

This compassionate self-acknowledgment may start out with a simple reflection: "I'm really uncomfortable when I visit Uncle Harry because he's suffering so much. I want so much to help him, but there doesn't seem to be anything I can do. I see how phony I get when I'm around him. And that's okay." But it's more than okay. This act of acknowledgment begins to go to work for us. The phoniness usually starts to fall away the minute it's owned up to. Discomfort in the presence of suffering is usually less toxic and infectious when it's no longer denied. This quality of unjudging awareness not only frees us and others from the consequences of our reactivity; it allows us to enter more consciously into the experience of suffering itself. We're no longer running away, glancing over our shoulder. We can stop and face what's right before us. We can look at *what is*.

But we must be quiet to do so, quiet to hear. Yet the first thing we notice when we try is that we're not quiet at all. We're a torrent of reactions, and reactions to reactions, one piling in upon the other. Such agitation is hardly the best ground from which to observe the subtleties of any situation. It would be so much easier if we weren't in the presence of all this suffering. But then again, wasn't it the suffering and our reactions to it that we set out to observe in the first place?

So we have to find tranquillity even in the midst of trauma. What's required is to cultivate a dispassionate Witness within. This Witness, as it grows stronger, can see precisely how we jump the gun in the presence of pain. It notices how our reactions might be perpetuating denial or fear or tension in the situation, the very qualities we'd like to help alleviate. The Witness catches us in the act, but gently, without reproach, so we can simply acknowledge our reactivity and begin to let it fall away, allowing our natural compassion to come more into play. The Witness gives us a little room.

Not only does it notice our own reactivity, but it also brings into the light of awareness the actions and reactions of other parties in the situation. Now we can begin, perhaps for the first time, to hear *them.* Less busy pushing away suffering, less frenzied having to do something about it, we're able to get a sense of what *they're* feeling, of what *they* feel they need. We may be startled to discover that what they've been asking for all along is entirely different from what we've been so busy offering: "All I want is for you to sit down here next to me. I don't care about the nurse; the IV is working fine; the bed is comfortable. Just sit with me." Quieter now, we can recognize such a need—often without it having to be expressed, perhaps even before it's consciously felt. We'll just come into the room and sit down and say "Hello."

This process of witnessing is dispassionate. It's not committed to one result or another; it's open to everything. Because it has, so to speak, no ax to grind, it is more able to see truth. As the Tao Te Ching says, "The truth waits for eyes unclouded by longing."

The Witness, however, is not passive, complacent, or indifferent. Indeed, while it's not attached to a particular outcome, its presence turns out to bring about change. As we bring *what is* into the light of clear awareness, we begin to see that the universe is providing us with abundant clues as to the nature of the suffering before us, what is being asked, what fears have been inhibiting us, and, finally, *what might really help*. All we have to do is listen—really listen.

Such investigation and inquiry into *what is* infuses a situation with a quality of freshness and possibility. As we see how reactive we have been, we find ourselves opening to new responses. It was our own reactivity unacknowledged that cut off the spontaneity of our helping heart. Once it is acknowledged, however—and once we begin to work with it—a whole new level of creativity becomes possible.

~

I used to have to walk through it automatically. You don't bother to look. You certainly don't let much of it in. But it was the children themselves who began to open me up. Once it started, it began to pull me in gradually but steadily. It was very powerful, but you have to take it at your own pace. Because here, in a neonatal intensive care unit, you see incredible beauty and unbearable pain. And you have to figure out how to be with both.

The children are beautiful because you just get to know them. You can't nurse them, really nurse them, without knowing them. And you can't know them, really know them, without seeing their beauty. What can be more beautiful than innocence? And that affects all their features: their tininess, the eyes, the fingers, the sound of their heart—just their breath can move you with its beauty. Part of it seems to come from how fragile they are, how uncer-

tain it is how long they'll be here—the cliché metaphor of the flower that blooms for a day. It's like a garden of that in here.

The picture on the surface, though, is also terribly grim. A room full of these little ones, many of whom are right on the edge of life and death, and some of whose faces and movements are pretty distressing. And then their parents: there on the other side of the window, with the most desperate and stricken faces looking in, so helplessly, such pain. It's something to be inside a picture that's being looked at with such expressions. But you look back, just to let them know someone's in here.

It was the use of machines and extraordinary medical measures that moved several of us to see how much distance we were putting between ourselves and the infants. Even if the machines weren't there, though, there was that tendency to keep it impersonal, to keep your distance, and you knew that wasn't any good for the children—for the children least of all.

So a group of us began to talk about it, to open up to our feelings, to decide to be with the children more, and when it got too hard and we'd break down, we'd support each other and talk it over. The more we opened up, it just became natural that we began this new practice of holding infants when the time would come for them to die. It wasn't a decision as much as something we'd become ready to do. So at the end we'd take them off the monitors and into our arms in a rocker. And we'd sit with them in their final moments.

It tears you apart, because holding them, sometimes you can feel them go. And the death itself is different. On the machines, it's monitored as brain death. In your arms, it's the heart and the breath.

It's so—what's that word?—poignant. You feel ten dozen things at once. Terrible sadness, because you'd become attached to the child. But glad too, because their suffering is about to end. Maybe anger, at the world, at God, at whatever, for allowing this to happen. And such empathy for the parents. And something like awe and wonder; like there must be some kind of explanation for all this which you don't yet understand. But patience too, that things become more clear in time. And peace of mind, because you're doing the best you can. And humble, to be present at such a moment. All of the above, often at once.

You're sitting with these feelings, as well as sitting there with the child. In fact, you come to see that you're sitting with all of it on behalf of the child. You're doing it for yourself, simply to stay cool. But it's a final act for them as well. You're offering whatever peace you've come to. And it creates such intimacy, impossible to describe, you're so right with them.

It's unbearable and beautiful at the same time. How do you explain that? It's just the part of you that's with them is getting ripped up. But the part of you that's, like, trying to understand it all . . . well, that's beautiful because you see that you can be, we all can be, in the presence of great pain, but still appreciate life, even in its last moments. Especially then.

~

Compassion follows lawfully as we open to the experience of suffering. Simply to observe and to open allows us to hear what is natural, harmonious, and appropriate. Instead of closed minds and mechanical reactions, there is open space and inventiveness. There is the helping of living truth.

So the activity of the quiet Witness not only shows us how fearfully reactive we have been to the suffering of others; it also releases within us a yearning to grow in our capacity to care for others. We look anew at how each situation can teach us, how it can help us evolve in our ability to confront and help alleviate suffering. We can be students working on ourselves to become more effective instruments of compassion.

The collaboration of the Witness and this yearning to grow, born of the inherent mercy of the heart, continues to bring to light patterns of response to suffering we hadn't noticed before. From situation to situation, we see these reactions repeated again and again. Sometimes they are appropriate. Very often they are unconscious. Instead of being responsive to an actual situation as it is, we come in with our reactions pretaped, just looking for ways to protect them. We may assume people are suffering in ways that they aren't: "Poor baby." "This must be awful for you." "Are you sure you don't want me to call someone?" "Take something for the pain." We wince when someone else gets an injection. We project discomfort onto people about their helplessness which doesn't necessarily exist, or we fail to see the character of the suffering that really is there.

As we begin to notice these tendencies in ourselves, we can look further and see where they come from, how we've built them up out of past experience. Certainly some have come from how we've dealt previously with the pain of others. But more significant still are our past experiences facing *our own* suffering. Here is the next critical issue we need to engage—one that any of us who seeks to help another must confront sooner or later.

~

My first visit to India included a stop at Benares. In the streets there were hundreds, perhaps thousands, of people with begging bowls who were in the final stages of one illness or another and seemed to be just waiting to die. My heart was deeply pained by the scene. I put lots of change in lots of begging bowls, but even then it didn't seem like enough. In encounters with these people I usually averted my eyes from meeting theirs. I guess I felt guilty that I had so much and they had so little. Finally I was remaining in the hotel rather than face such massive suffering.

By the time of my next visit to the city many months later, I had become familiar with the Hindu culture. I now realized that Benares was one of the most sacred cities in India, situated on the banks of the Ganges, the most sacred river. I also had come to know that in this culture, which believed so deeply in reincarnation, the most auspicious place to die was in Benares. To be cremated there on the river bank assured liberation after death. Now as I placed coins in begging bowls I was able to look into the eyes of the people. And to my profound amazement I found in their eyes not the suffering that I had been reticent to face but looks of peace. In fact I even saw in some of their eyes pity for me, lost as I was in illusion. Leprosy, leukemia, blindness, such poverty that they had only a loincloth and begging bowl . . . and still . . . peace. How wrong I'd been to assume that they were suffering as I would have been suffering in a similar situation.

~

The link between our reaction to our own pain and the quality of our empathy for that of others needs to be examined carefully. The more we understand it, the deeper, freer, more naturally compassionate our response to the pain we all experience at one time or another.

What causes suffering for us in the first place? An unpleasant sensation or situation arises. It could be physical pain, psychological distress, general uncertainty about the future, and so forth. These are potential conditions for suffering. But taken alone, these are not the suffering itself. *How we react to them* determines how much we will suffer. These reactions can vary.

A child and an adult each stub a toe. They both experience pain. The adult has a world view in which such sensation is recognized and incorporated: it's one of those things, it'll pass. So the adult experiences the sensation of pain but does not really "suffer" beyond that. Because there is no uncontrolled reactive resistance to speak of, the adult need initiate no action to alleviate the "suffering."

For the child the experience is quite different. Lacking a context that readily allows for stubbed toes, the child *identifies* with the unpleasant pain and experiences aversion to it. The child puts itself strongly at odds with *what is*. This resistance to the unpleasant situation is the root of the suffering. Tears may continue after the sensation has subsided. As a reaction, the child runs to the parent for solace.

Two people have not eaten in three days. One is a yogi

doing a purification fast. Though there are unpleasant sensations in the stomach, there is very little aversion, perhaps even none, hence little or no real suffering. The yogi sits quietly and takes no steps to change the state of affairs.

Another person, however, lives on the street, has no job, no food stamps, and hasn't eaten in three days. The unpleasant sensations are painful, and their causes add to them a strong element of suffering: frustration, anger, humiliation. He's suffering. He goes out begging.

Two women are in labor. They're both screaming as a natural response to pain. For one of them the pain represents the heralding of the long-awaited child and is part of the incredible mystery of life. The pain draws her in and fills her not with suffering but with ecstasy. She has never felt so alive and in such deep harmony with her nature. She rejects a pain killer solicitously offered by the midwife.

For the other woman, the pain of childbirth is what she's been afraid of since the onset of pregnancy. When it arises, she is unable to push it away. It becomes a source of suffering, not part of an experience of overall joy. She welcomes the pain medication.

How dramatic, then, the range of potential reactions among us to unpleasant circumstances, whatever their form. Down with a cold? Is it a fearful intimation of mortality or a chance just to let go for a few days? Newly divorced? Do you feel rejected or acknowledge the opportunity to be free of accumulated dependencies? Just fired from work? Are you worthless or free to discover new skills?

Obviously, certain circumstances or sensations are more likely to trigger off greater suffering than others. But suffering can exist even without immediate or proximate cause. We experience it frequently in this general, floating form. We simply want things to be other than they are. What we have . . . isn't quite enough. Who we are . . . isn't quite satisfactory. How we feel . . . could always be a little better. That which is . . . just isn't right.

In the face of unpleasant circumstance or experience, then, it is often the context, framework, or disposition of mind that determines the extent to which there is suffering.

We hear stories of great tribulation. A man in great pain with advanced cancer is now denied the strength he always had as a professional carpenter, a supportive husband, and a father of four. A teen-ager is hurt in an automobile crash and has lost the use of both legs. A woman is told she can never have children; she's become alcoholic; they've just fired her from her job. We can easily feel in ourselves the likely reactions such people must experience under such conditions.

~

~ *My God, I can't believe this is happening to me!*
~ *I'm so totally unprepared.*
~ *I'll never be the same.*
~ *My life's a failure.*
~ *Everywhere I look now, I only see reason for despair.*
~ *I just plain feel sorry for myself, that's all.*
~ *I feel trapped in this useless body.*
~ *Helpless, utterly helpless . . .*

~ *I want to scream and I can't.*
~ *What did I do to deserve this?*
~ *I'll never make it through another day.*
~ *I don't want to hear about anybody else's problems.*
~ *Everyone is a stranger. I feel totally alone.*
~ *I keep expecting to wake up and be healed.*
~ *Why me?*

~

Our hearts go out to these people, not only because of the immediate circumstances but because, intuitively, we recognize the response of mental suffering that we ourselves would experience under such conditions. Their predicament awakens our own fears of pain or loss of control. It's so easy to empathize with their reactions of resistance.

But it also must be said that other people respond to such trying circumstances differently. While this may happen as a result of remarkable personal growth, forged by the crucible of affliction, we can hear in their responses the possibility that extreme pain need not always be intimately associated with extreme suffering.

~

It stinks, it's terrible. But it is what it is, and I'm going to go on living with it for however long I have.

~

When your negligence has resulted in someone's death, I can't describe the amount of guilt you feel. And then a moment comes when you move from utter humiliation to sim-

ple humility. It's your fault, but also somehow it isn't. We live lives where such things happen. And in that moment you begin to forgive yourself. You don't deny what you've done. You pass through it, it rips you up, and you come out the other end—with a new possibility that comes from that humility and self-forgiveness.

~

As long as I was pushing away the pain, it had me nailed to the wall. But then I stopped resisting it. I sort of let it in. It was actually a relief. I felt better in spite of it. No longer at odds with everything.

~

When my daughter was murdered, I felt unbearable anguish. I couldn't sleep, eat, anything. And then a friend and I prayed together. At one moment I felt God's mercy. Even though I couldn't understand this crazy mess, I had a sense that there was something behind it all that made it . . . meaningful. After that, the hurt didn't go away, but it was bearable.

~

We hear in these testimonies something else with which we can empathize: the possibility of coming up for air even in the midst of the most painful, even agonizing, conditions. Somehow we sense that we could be with pain in some way so as not to be suffering so much. Just as we have known in ourselves the fear and resistance, so we have also had moments when we have experienced pain, yet transcended suffering.

Just the possibility that such pain need not automatically cause continuous suffering is profoundly important. This possibility, in fact, was the foundation stone of the teachings of the Buddha. He saw that if we could break that link between painful conditions and the reactiveness of mind there was hope of liberating ourselves from the continuous experience of suffering. He realized that pain alone is not the enemy; the real enemy is fear and resistance.

It's not difficult to recognize how deep are the ways our mind has been conditioned to deal with unpleasant situations by resisting them. Throughout our whole lives we have been encouraged to do anything we can to escape from rather than to explore and investigate unpleasantness. Our society consumes literally tons of aspirin daily. It's not just physical pain we try to avoid, but all kinds of unpleasant conditions: boredom, restlessness, self-doubt, anger, loneliness, loss, feelings of unworthiness. In our culture we do all we can to push these experiences aside, or keep them at a distance. We choose to be entertained.

So it gets to the point that the slightest unpleasantness elicits our push against it. We tense in opposition. As the unpleasantness gets stronger, the opposition becomes more formidable. Our hearts are closed down by the fear in our minds—fear of loss of control, of being overwhelmed, ultimately of extinction. Our muscles tighten, our energies become knotted and blocked. And, of course, if suddenly we are hit by enormous affliction and adversity, we've no habits except resistance.

Under these conditions, to suggest that we turn around and look at what so frightens us—to open a dialogue with the enemy rather than just piling up the sandbags and amassing arsenals—is asking us to go in the face of all our conditioning. It is asking us to walk intentionally to the edge of unexplored territory, to relate to the unknown. No small task. Imagine yourself in a state of pain you particularly fear, really fear, being asked to explore it, investigate it, even somehow make friends with it. Just the thought of it can awaken a dread that reveals the potential enormity of our opposition.

Yet many have found that it is possible at least to *begin* such a process—to face the pain, not defiantly, but gently, with close attention and compassion for ourselves. Perhaps we've gone through a divorce and felt the terrible sting of rejection. We've lost a partner to death and felt the sudden onslaught of grief. We've experienced periods of deep self-doubt or feelings of unworthiness. We've just felt deeply depressed by a sense of great separateness from others, cut off, alone, barely touching when we do meet.

While we'd just as soon deny our pain because it's too searing, at a certain point we've turned to face it and explore what it is that we are really feeling. This is the beginning of constructive work. We cease resisting and begin to open. In that action we introduce some space into the situation—the space between the pain and our suffering reaction. In that awareness, we see that what we imagined to be unbearable is potentially bearable. There are alternative responses to pain other than resistant reactivity. There are ways to cultivate this space systematically. Certain meditations for opening around pain, whether physical or psychological, assist us in this effort. An example of one of these might help make this process more vivid.

OPENING TO PAIN

Find a position in which you can remain comfortable and quiet for a few minutes.

Bring into your awareness a thought or a bodily sensation that is unpleasant to you. Perhaps it may be an image or memory, a physical pain or ache. Choose only one.

Let your attention settle around this thought or sensation.

Allow yourself to be with the discomfort.

Bring your attention ever more intimately to bear on the thought or sensation.

Feel the way in which your mind or body tends to push against the unpleasantness, to close it off.

Feel in your mind or in your body both the pain and the resistance against the pain: both present . . . yet separate from one another.

Notice your tendency to want to identify with the resistance and to deny or isolate or push away the pain.

But instead of reactively pushing the painful thought or sensation away, stay with it . . . gently but firmly.

Now start to loosen the ring of resistance that surrounds the painful thought or sensation, loosening its hold in the same way you might allow a fist to open.

Consider the possibility that the resistance to the pain may be more painful than the pain itself. Notice how the resistance closes your heart and fills your body and mind with tension and dis-ease.

Keep relaxing the resistance . . . the tightness . . . that have accumulated around the pain.

Notice any fear that has developed around this unpleasant thought or sensation. Allow the fear to melt . . . to dissolve . . . along with the resistance . . . softening . . . opening . . . releasing. . . .

Let the painful thought or sensation float free . . . no longer held in the grasp of resistance.

Keep letting go of any resistance that tries to smother the experience. Allow the unpleasant thoughts or sensations to come fully into consciousness. No holding . . . no pushing away . . . just floating free. . . .

All grasping relinquished. Just the thought or sensation, and the awareness of it . . . together . . . moment to moment.

See that the unpleasant thought is just a thought . . . the painful sensation is just a sensation . . . just that . . . nothing more. . . .

Softening . . . opening . . . releasing . . . allowing . . . again and again . . . until there is just thought . . . just sensation. . . .

And it keeps changing . . . from moment to moment . . . it always keeps changing. . . .

Soft . . .

    open . . .

        gentle . . .

            allowing . . .

                floating free. . . .

adapted from *Who Dies,* STEPHEN LEVINE

Whether the pain is physical or psychological, the fist that is tightened around it can loosen. As we have been conditioned, so we can be deconditioned, so we can discover the possibility of freedom. As we play the edge of our pain—gently opening, acknowledging, and allowing—the suffering it has caused diminishes. If we further dissolve the boundaries, letting ourselves enter into the pain and the pain enter into us, we can see the possibility of going beyond it to where the heart is freer. We've never been so vulnerable, so defenseless, and yet somehow so safe. The surrender we were so frightened of turns out to be not defeat but a kind of victory.

Or at the very least an opening. We should never underestimate the difficulty of this process, at any time, under any circumstances. It is nothing to hurl at one another—"Open to your pain!"—as if it didn't require great patience and discipline, a willingness to fail, fall, and try once more. The practice is not heartless, not rooted in any kind of denial of what's entailed. It is a practice of compassion *for ourselves*—the very same attentive listening and patient open-heartedness we would eagerly offer another.

Opening to our pain, exploring the roots of our suffering, at best with guidance or support, can always increase our opportunity for well-being. But this process also can be of immeasurable value in our efforts to be of service to others. As our understanding of our own suffering deepens, we become available at deeper levels to those we would care for. We are less likely to project suffering that does not exist or deny that which does. We're much more sensitive and alert to the nuances of human pain.

We do not, however, insist that others go to the edge of their own pain. Under no circumstances do we judge or condemn another's suffering. We merely continue to work on our own, steadily, continuously, in all areas of our life. Opening to adversity and discovering in it all the places where we are clinging, resisting and denying, we gradually cut the cord between pain and suffering. The pain is there, but we can move beyond the suffering. To the extent that we ourselves are free of suffering, our very being becomes an environment in which others can be free of theirs, if it is in the way of things.

It is in just this manner that the great spiritual teachers have perennially been of help to humankind. The power of their compassion has been rooted in the fact that they themselves have overcome the entrapment of suffering. They have broken the link between painful circumstance and mental resistance. They have gone beyond it. This doesn't mean that they have denied the experience of pain. In Gethsemane, on the cross, throughout his life, Christ surely felt and understood the burden of human incarnation. In his humanity, he experienced it. But in his divinity, he transcended it and transformed it into redemption and liberation, a possibility for all. So too the Buddha, having seen what he saw, could look across all the fields of human existence with "the Smile of Unbearable Compassion." We can feel this same quality of compassion, which combines fully experiencing but also transcending suffering, in the story of the great Tibetan teacher Marpa, who lived on a farm with his family but welcomed many seekers and monks who came to him for instruction and wisdom.

~

One day, Marpa's eldest son was killed. Off by himself, alone with his grief, Marpa wept. One of his students approached him and said, "I don't understand. You teach that all this is illusion, created by the clinging and desire and resistance. Yet here you are weeping. If all this is illusion, why do you grieve so deeply?"

Marpa replied, "Yes, everything here is an illusion. And the death of a child is the greatest of these illusions."

~

For us, then, investigation of the causes of suffering within is a tool. Here is our work; here is the path. We conduct the journey according to our own individual temperament and intuition. No one can force us to do this. It's ours to undertake or not, as appropriate. But it can be of equal value in moments when we are helping others and those in which we ourselves are seeking or receiving care. At times we will be able to break the conditioning of mind and let go of the suffering. At other times, until our self-investigative practice is highly developed, we are bound to get lost in resistance to pain.

So we work to understand suffering itself—not just the conditions which give rise to it but the nature of our various reactions to it as well. The range turns out to be vast. Some of us become obsessed by our suffering; others try to ignore it. Some curl up in the fetal position and withdraw into themselves; others wander about confused, grabbing at straws in the wind. Some keep businesslike; others childishly irresponsible. Some keep a stiff upper lip; others cry and turn to jelly.

Habitual reactions also include the way we respond to help from others. When in pain, we may reach for help swiftly or spurn any aid. We may be embarrassed at discovering our need or assume it is our right to demand help aggressively. We may feel we have been wronged or are being punished by suffering and become angry or play martyr, or we may be softened by pain and receive support graciously.

For one receiving help, it can be immensely useful to become more conscious of the habitual ways in which we react to our suffering and the help offered to alleviate it. Just seeing these patterns clearly may allow us to discard reactions that cut us off from others at a time when we need them the most.

For one who is seeking to offer help, investigation of our habitual reactions to our own suffering can illuminate the subtle ways in which we may judge others for theirs. Many helpers, when they themselves are suffering, are incapable of accepting support, or at least receiving it easily. Yet they may be impatient with those they're working with for not accepting aid or counsel readily enough. Chances are, if you can't accept help, you can't really give it.

While all of this is an extremely complicated psychodynamic interaction, one thing seems obvious. The more conscious we are in dealing with our own suffering, the more sensitive we will be in treating the pain of others.

~

I have a friend, a chemotherapy nurse in a children's cancer ward, whose job it is to pry for any available vein in an often emaciated arm to give infusions of chemicals that sometimes last as long as twelve hours and which are often quite discomforting to the child. He is probably the greatest pain giver the children meet in their stay in the hospital. Because he has worked so much with his own pain, his heart is very open. He works with his responsibilities in the hospital as a "laying on of hands with love and acceptance." There is little in him that causes him to withdraw, that reinforces the painfulness of the experience for the children. He is a warm, open space which encourages them to trust whatever they feel. And it is he whom the children most often ask for at the time they are dying. Although he is the main pain-giver, he is also the main love-giver.

~

What objectives can we set, what resources can we call upon then in the great effort to relieve suffering? First we must face it and let it in. Different orders of service and loving kindness follow.

Our immediate responsibility is to do what we can to alleviate the concrete conditions of human affliction. We work to provide food for the hungry, shelter for the homeless, health care for the sick and feeble, protection for the threatened and vulnerable, schooling for the un-educated, freedom for the oppressed. *To this order of service we must always attend first.*

Where we cannot help provide such aid, we may be called on to offer a different kind of support. Perhaps we can help another to reperceive his or her situation so that while it is unpleasant or painful, he or she need suffer less as a reaction to it. This can't take the form of facile counsel. Such support can come only from the truth of our own being. However much we have been able to break our own reactiveness to pain, however well we have cultivated those qualities of mind and heart that allow us to be open to affliction yet not be reactive to it, we will have that to offer others. The right form, the right words, the right moment, will all follow. At this stage, we do not *have* help to *give,* we *are* help itself.

Even in those situations where another person is completely enmeshed in the web of a suffering mind and is not receptive to help in reperceiving the situation, we can be of comfort. We can offer our own empathy, our own experience, our own understanding of how it feels when we suffer: the resistance, tension, fear, withdrawal, self-pity, doubt, the utter separateness. This compassion will guide our helping hand to appropriate gestures: a simple word of friendship to cut through the isolation; a gentle neck massage to ease the tension; a tender hug or touch to convey love; a meeting of the eyes for a moment beyond it all.

Sometimes we may be able to do all these things at once: nourish the hungry stomach, the famished heart, and the yearning soul. But perhaps there will be nothing we can *do.* Then we can only *be,* and *be with* the person in his or her pain, attending to the quality of our *own* consciousness. On his or her behalf, we will dwell in whatever truth and understanding we have come to which is beyond suffering. From this, compassion arises. Hearts that have known pain meet in mutual recognition and trust. Such a meeting helps immeasurably.

~

When I left New York harbor for Peru, I instinctively felt I was making a journey that would shape my life. It was 1951; I was robust and eager. I wasn't even sure what my real mission would be. At that point, there was just an empty lot.

It was thirteen thousand five hundred feet high, very cold and demanding. As a Maryknoll sister, I was there to teach school. After a while I became principal. I guess you could say I was a figure, just by being in that role. Then the illness happened, quite suddenly, up there. The doctors said it was rheumatoid arthritis. They said it was ultimately a crippling disease. They said there was nothing really to do about it.

I went to see other doctors elsewhere, like in Panama, because I wanted to stay in South America. I wouldn't accept what they were telling me, what I was going to have to face. But it gradually became clear I should come back to the States for some treatment.

I got good care. However, the doctors said that gold injections would be the only help, but it would prevent me from going back to Peru. I didn't want them. I was going back. I was fighting it, fighting it all—the illness, my own reactions—self-pity, anger, discouragement, doubt. I wouldn't give in. But every day it seemed I was losing. Finally I felt I had to quit imposing my own will; that was a big step. I went to the doctors, and they said they could give me this medicine, and after a few months they'd see if I could get onto maintenance and go back to Peru. After all my anger and resistance, there seemed to be some kind of chance. But chance for what?

I had surgery at the Mayo Clinic, and I did a great deal of reflecting and praying in their chapel. There was a beautiful wooden statue of Christ there, with outstretched hands. I think that's why it had been chosen, to inspire the hands of surgeons and nurses. As it happened I was there to have my own hands operated on. I remember thinking that even though my hands were going to be broken and crooked, they would still be sacred to me. I'd use them to bring something to somebody, I didn't know what. My hands could be the compassionate hands of Christ as much as the hands of the doctors and nurses.

So I sought to be able to enter into the world of the sick, and to live with the mystery of suffering. I saw that I had to enter into my own experience of pain, and to face up to it, and to allow myself to be changed by it. Without that nothing could be done. I saw that healing comes with owning our wounds as the first step in moving beyond them.

I returned to Peru at a lower altitude. Almost everything had changed, especially my attitude toward the people I was working with. I could feel their terrible poverty and pain in a whole new way. In fact it seemed as if I was seeing it for the first time. How often I'd rushed around trying to solve people's problems without really seeing them—the pain in their faces, the insecure eyes, the nervous hands, all expressions of the hurt inside. It was only when suffering had actually touched me that I began to feel their condition.

The affirmation I got from them was so important: "You're the same person you were before. And even if you can't teach or do anything, we'd like you to stay." Just to see me get up and try to do something seemed to mean a great deal to them. We were meeting on a level where we all suffer. That became our ground.

And so my ministry changed. It became the ministry of walking together. Some of us with physical disabilities joined together to share our experiences. We were just being *together, trying to understand what was possible for us, share what we could, examples of creativity. Our pain and weakness and deformity proved to be teachers of a great mystery, a small introduction into the kind of dying from which new spirit is born.*

We found we had become more sensitive to others, more touched, more able to listen, moved more by feelings than by intellectual concepts. We discovered that the more we opened to the pain of others, the more we found ourselves in their service. Having been brought low, it was just a matter of standing humbly before others, and presenting a visible sign of hope by some silent testimony.

So we would simply walk about, as best we could. Many of the Peruvians we ran into with handicaps were deeply ashamed and hid. We would come to see them, and they would hide, in their own homes. But as we moved about, they would gradually come forth more.

I think of Juan, a polio victim at three, who had been hidden by his family in their small mud-brick house until we discovered him at the age of eight. His brother, Julio, took us home one day. There was Juan, his twisted legs underneath him, scooting around the small dirt patio on a circular piece of rubber. His mother was suspicious and didn't want us to stay. A handicapped child meant she was being punished for something. She was ashamed.

We returned on several occasions to visit Juan. One time we found him all alone. His family, with the rest of the town, had gone to a religious procession. Of course, he'd never seen one. So we borrowed a bicycle, put Juan on it, and joined in the procession itself. It was his first time outside the house, the first time he'd looked at people from a level higher than the ground, his first procession.

His parents were momentarily annoyed, but their attitude changed gradually. When we thought it was right to raise the idea, we asked at the next town meeting if we could raise money to send Juan to Lima for physical rehabilitation. Everyone liked the idea and Juan went off to the big city.

He had a long, hard struggle, with much pain and effort. But one day he returned to the village. He was using braces and a cane. It was very hard for him. But as he began to walk down the streets to his home, people came out of their own homes. They appeared from all over. They were cheering and clapping and they followed him all the way home. It was so wonderful. It was Juan's second procession.

It's difficult. I have had many ups and downs. That's the thing about a progressive crippling disease: more and more pain and disability; it keeps on pushing you, making more demands, forcing you to greater discipline.

But I have seen much service born of suffering. And I see that our little suffering is not for ourselves. It can have impact throughout the world, that's how much our lives can mean, that's how much is possible. And I have been with people who would just cry over that message, cry and cry. And I have cried too.

4

The Listening Mind

Much of our capacity to help another person depends upon our state of mind. Sometimes our minds are so scattered, confused, depressed, or agitated, we can hardly get out of bed. At other times we're clear, alert, and receptive; we feel ready, even eager, to respond generously to the needs of others. Most of the time it's really not one extreme or the other. Our minds are . . . well . . . they're just our minds. Like old cars, typewriters, or appliances, we put up with their idiosyncrasies with a shrug. What can we do about it anyway?

Perhaps we settle for too little. Our mind, after all, is our most potentially powerful tool. With it we have harnessed fire, devised technology, extended our ability to grow and process food, developed ways to protect ourselves from the elements, discovered means to cure illness and extend our life span.

Our mind is not only the source of ideas, a tool for gathering data, an instrument of training and technique, or a repository of experience and memory. Because the mind's capacity to think is so brilliant, we tend to be dazzled by it and fail to notice other attributes and functions. There is more to the mind than reason alone. There is *awareness itself* and what we sometimes think of as the deeper *qualities* of mind. Most of us know how supportive it is merely to be in the presence of a mind that is open, quiet, playful, receptive, or reflective. These attributes are *themselves* helpful. Moreover, there is something we frequently experience—perhaps we can call it intuitive awareness—that links us most intimately to the universe and, in allegiance with the heart, binds us together in generosity and compassion. Often it leaps to vision and knowledge instantaneously. "My understanding of the fundamental laws of the universe," said Albert Einstein, "did not come out of my rational mind."

This resource of awareness can give us access to deeper power, power to help and heal.

~

I had been meditating for a number of years. My progress, in terms of increased concentration and a more peaceful, quiet quality in my mind, was noticeable, though not dramatic. In the ancient texts I'd read accounts of monks who through meditation had gained great powers, and I kept wondering if the stories were true.

Then, I visited the wife of the former American ambassador in Thailand, and she told me about a monk who had built a monastery in which heroin and opium addicts were cured in ten days ... for fifteen dollars. These kinds of statistics are unheard of in the West. Possibly this was one of those monks with the meditation powers. I prevailed on her to take me to meet him.

The monk had previously been a Thai "narc" . . . something like our federal drug enforcement agency. He had an aunt who I was told was a Buddhist saint, whatever that means. One day she apparently said to him, while he was still a narc, "What are you doing? If you don't watch out you're going to end up killing people in this job. Why don't you help these people instead of hurting them?" He said that he didn't know how. She apparently told him to clean up his act and she'd show him.

So he left government service and became a monk. Now the Buddhist monks in Thailand are part of the Theravadin tradition which requires very severe renunciation in order to purify your mind so that you can do deep meditation. There are some two hundred and eighteen prohibitions, all of which he adopted. Then he even added ten more on his own, such as never driving in automobiles. This meant that when he had business in Bangkok, about a hundred and fifty miles away, he'd just pick up his walking stick and start walking.

This rigorous training prepared him to do very intensive meditation practice which allowed him to tune to the deeper and more powerful parts of his mind. When his aunt felt he was ready, she instructed him in the preparation of an herbal diuretic which she instructed him to give to the addicts, and he started his monastery.

When we met him, my most immediate reaction was that I was shaking hands with an oak tree. His presence was immensely powerful and solid. He had us shown through the monastery where some three hundred addicts were undergoing treatment.

*You could really see who was which. The first-day arriv-
als all looked like strung-out junkies. They were in one
room. Then, further on, by the time they had been there for
four days you could really see a change. And by eight days
they seemed cheerful, were bumming cigarettes from me,
and seemed really friendly—not particularly like addicts at
all. And then after ten days they were gone. And their statistics showed seventy percent remained free of addiction
afterwards. Amazing.*

*When I interviewed the monk, I asked him, "How do you
do it?" He said, "Well, it's simple. I tell them that they can
only come for ten days and they may never come again,
and that the cure will work." I asked him if a lot of religious
indoctrination was included in the ten-day program. "No,"
he said, "none of that. These people aren't suitable for
that."*

*I had heard that many drug experts, media people, and
even some congressmen had come from the West, but that
none of them could figure out why what he did worked.
The herbal brew clearly wasn't the whole ballgame. As I
hung out with him longer I began to realize that his mind
was so centered and one-pointed that his being was stronger
than their addiction. Somehow he conveyed to those addicts a sense of their non-addiction that was stronger than
their addiction. And I saw that his commitment was so
total, that he wasn't just someone using a skill. He had died
into his work. He was the cure.*

*This was the example I had been looking for. Just being
with him I could feel the extraordinary quality of his mind.
Meeting him reassured me that the ancient stories were
probably true. I returned to meditation with renewed vigor.*

~

Most of us are not really ready to become renunciates in order to develop the concentration and quality of awareness necessary to help others at such an extraordinary level. But if we are prepared to investigate our minds even a little bit, we start a process that can improve our effectiveness in life, and therefore in helping as well. If we are willing to examine the agitation of our own minds and look just beyond it, we quite readily find entry into rooms that hold surprising possibilities: a greater inner calm, sharper concentration, deeper intuitive understanding, and an enhanced ability to hear one another's heart. Such an inquiry turns out to be critical in the work of helping others.

The phone rings. We turn from the checkbook we were balancing to answer. It's someone seeking counsel. Even as the person begins to speak, our minds are conflicted. We don't quite want to leave that column of figures unadded, and yet we know that we have to let go of our bookkeeping to listen carefully to the problem.

The voice on the other end tries to find words to describe suffering: "I'm just feeling so . . . it's like I . . . I really don't know, but. . . ." Painstaking work. But sometimes even as it starts, our mind may begin to wander. "This is going to be a tough one. . . . Am I up to this? . . . What about dinner? . . . I'd better circle that place where I think the bank screwed up."

At a certain stage, personal judgments may start competing for attention. "He's really romanticizing it a lot. . . . He ought to be done with this one by now. . . . He's not hearing what I mean." We may get a little lost in evaluating—"Is it working? Am I helping?" Or we could as easily turn the evaluation on ourselves, "I don't care that much. I really don't like him."

Sometimes we catch ourselves in distraction and rejoin the person on the other end of the phone. Now it's better. Something's beginning to happen. Then we take an intentionally audible in-breath—we've got something helpful to say—but the signal goes by; he keeps right on talking. Off goes the mind to utterly unrelated topics: "Call Dad. . . . That picture on the wall is crooked. . . . I'm tired. . . . I have to feed the cat."

This mental chatter goes on and off. Sometimes we really get lost, and by the time we're back, we realize we've missed a key point, and it's too late to ask for it to be repeated. At other times we can take quick note of our reactions and still stay with it. Perhaps we just let it all run off; it's not something we even notice—it fades into the background like film-score music we're hardly aware is there.

Then the call is over. The voice on the other end says "Thank you." We reply "You're welcome." But how welcome was he? How much room did the mind give him? How much did we really hear? How much did he *feel* heard? Maybe we sit back in the chair and reflect on that for a moment. Or perhaps we get up, walk to the kitchen, and savor the "thank you" along with a sandwich. Perhaps we simply turn back to the checkbook.

Reckoning, judging, evaluating, leaping in, taking it personally, being bored—the helping act has any number of invitations to reactiveness and distraction. Partly we are agitated because we so intensely want to help.

After all, someone's in pain. We care. So part of the time we are listening, but we may also be using our minds to try to solve the problem. There's a pull to be efficient, to look for some kind of resolution. We reach for certain familiar models or approaches. In order to be helpful, our analytic mind must stay on top of it all.

So we jump between listening and judging. But in our zeal to help, we may increase the distance between the person and our own consciousness. We find ourselves primarily in our own thoughts, not *with* another person. Not only are we listening less, but the concepts our mind is coming up with start to act as a screen that preselects information. One thought rules out another.

One of the results of all this mental activity is that there's less room to meet, less room for a new truth to emerge, less room to let things simply be revealed in "their own good time." The mind tries to do too many things at once. It's difficult to know which mental vectors are useful and which are distractions, static on the line, bad connections.

This agitation and reactiveness should be no surprise to most of us. We have come to expect and accept this state except in rare situations. Yet it need not be that way.

~

A big, tough samurai once went to see a little monk. "Monk," he said, in a voice accustomed to instant obedience, "teach me about heaven and hell!"

The monk looked up at this mighty warrior and replied with utter disdain, "Teach you about heaven and hell? I couldn't teach you about anything. You're dirty. You

smell. Your blade is rusty. You're a disgrace, an embarrass-
ment to the samurai class. Get out of my sight. I can't stand
you."

The samurai was furious. He shook, got all red in the
face, was speechless with rage. He pulled out his sword and
raised it above him, preparing to slay the monk.

"That's hell," said the monk softly.

The samurai was overwhelmed. The compassion and sur-
render of this little man who had offered his life to give this
teaching to show him hell! He slowly put down his sword,
filled with gratitude, and suddenly peaceful.

"And that's heaven," said the monk softly.

~

If we continue to observe our mind over some time, we
notice that it's not always distracted and busy. For all of
us, there are times when our minds become concen-
trated, sharp and clear. Perhaps we are doing a cross-
word puzzle, playing a video game, reading a mystery
story, cleaning house or cooking. For some, it's the simple
tasks that engage us in ways that allow our mind to be
composed and focused; for others, it's complex problem
solving.

Many times, however, the needs of others are what
bring us to a state of sharp concentration. Whether it's
because we feel very secure with those we're with or because we are functioning under conditions of extreme
crisis, we find that in this state of intense concentration
helpful insights arise on their own, as a function of our
one-pointedness. In these experiences we meet a resource
of remarkable potential. While we may be frustrated in
not having access to it all the time, these experiences lead

us to inquire whether there might be something we could do more regularly and formally to quiet the mind, strengthen its concentration, make available the deeper insights that often result, and bring them into closer attunement with the empathy and compassion of our heart. How immeasurably this might enhance our ability to help others.

Traditionally, one such way to begin this investigation is through meditation, systematically observing the mind itself and becoming more familiar with the ways in which we are denied the experience of full concentration. When we do this, with even a simple exercise like focusing our attention on our breath or on a candle flame, we begin to see that there is a continuous stream of thoughts going on all the time. Meditation may be frustrating if we think we can stop this process right away. We can't. But by penetrating and observing it, we can free ourselves from being carried away by our thoughts.

Our thoughts are always happening. Much like leaves floating down a stream or clouds crossing the sky, they just keep on coming. They arise in the form of sensations, feelings, memories, anticipations, and speculations. And they are all constantly calling for attention: "Think of me." "Notice me." "Attend to me." As each thought passes, either we attend to it or we don't. While we can't stop the thoughts themselves, we can stop our awareness from being snared by each one. If you are standing by a river and a leaf floats by, you have your choice of following the leaf with your eye or keeping your attention fixed in front of you. The leaf floats out of your line of vision. Another leaf enters . . . and floats by.

But as we stand on the bank of the river and the leaves

float by, there is no confusion as to whether or not we *are* the leaves. Similarly, it turns out that there is a place in our minds from which we can watch our own mental images go by. We aren't our thoughts any more than we are the leaves.

If we imagine that our mind is like the blue sky, and that across it pass thoughts as clouds, we can get a feel for that part of it which is other than our thoughts. The sky is always present; it contains the clouds and yet is not contained by them. So with our awareness. It is present and encompasses all our thoughts, feelings, and sensations; yet it is not the same as them. To recognize and acknowledge this awareness, with its spacious, peaceful quality, is to find a very useful resource within. We see that we need not identify with each thought just because it happens to occur. We can remain quiet and choose which thought we wish to attend to. And we can remain aware *behind* all these thoughts, in a state that offers an entirely new level of openness and insight.

There are systematic exercises that can help to establish us in the skylike awareness that encompasses thought. One of these meditation exercises is called "Letting Go." It very quickly can show us through direct personal experience that our awareness is separate from our thoughts. You may want to read it through until you understand it, and then, if you choose, try it.

LETTING GO

Find a position in which you can comfortably remain for ten minutes with your back straight but not rigid. This time, instead of picking an object of focus such as the breath, just observe thought itself. Simply let things happen as they do. Just watch. Be aware, as thoughts arise, that the thoughts are there, without getting involved in the content of the thoughts. Let all images, thoughts, and sensations arise and pass away without being bothered, without reacting, without judging, without clinging, without identifying with them. Just keep letting go of one thing after another.

The thoughts that arise are not obstacles or hindrances. They are just the objects of our observation. Keep the mind sharply aware, moment to moment, of what is happening, what the mind is attending to. If you feel tense from trying to watch your mind, relax. The sky doesn't get all tense trying to see the clouds. Everything is just as it is.

Keep in mind the idea of letting go. As thoughts or sensations, images, memories, whatever, rise into your awareness, notice them, witness them, and then let them go. Keep letting go again and again. And of course, once you are really comfortable and at home in pure awareness, then you can let go of the thought of letting go as well.

For one who has not examined the mind and has always identified completely with passing thoughts, the possibility of being able to rest in awareness free of thought may be a bit disconcerting. It's a little like the caterpillar pointing up at the butterfly and saying, "You'll never get me up in one of those things."

While we rarely are able to maintain this kind of awareness all the time, we have all experienced it at one time or another.

You're waiting tables, say, at a busy restaurant, setting one and clearing another, swinging through the kitchen door with an order and a funny remark for the cooks, then coming back out with a trayful and noticing what else needs to be done. The group of eight is eager to order, but they just sat down. The couple in the corner is stretching out their coffee while other folks are on line. It seems right to stop by and say, "Anything else?"

Or you're teaching in a nursery school. You've got your eye on the whole room. The boys are hogging the blocks from a couple of girls, as usual. Three kids over there are struggling a little over who's going to use the two easels. Janet hasn't played with anyone this morning, but she's better off working it out herself. Marc looks a little blue . . . you'd best spend time with him right now.

We're doing it all, attending to obvious needs, but we're also behind it. The consciousness we have access to is greater than the particular thoughts we're having or skills we've mastered. We have all these. But we have perspective as well—all within our spacious awareness. What's crucial is that this awareness allows us to hear, along with everything else, whatever it is that's going on inside us. *Our own mental reactions are equally objects to be observed as anything else in our field of awareness.* So you notice that perhaps you pushed the couple with the coffee just a little too much. You can see they're talking over something important. As you pass by, then, you say quietly,

"Take a few more minutes; it's okay." Or you recognize, as you decide where to put your energies in the classroom, that you're really quite fascinated by Marc; that's why you want to work with him. And you're not all that crazy about Janet. You reconsider where to spend your time.

In skillful helping action, when our awareness remains quiet and clear, there's breadth to our perspective. It's aerial, wide-screen, panoramic, and yet able to focus quickly. With all of this, we are not only thinker-participants but observers of our thinking and participation as well. It's as if our mind is playing among various focal lengths. We're watching a TV show and we pull back; it becomes a show within a show, a picture of a picture, both on simultaneously. Of course, that's true of who we are too. We're not only a person, say, walking down a city street at night; we're also, as it were, already home in bed watching the TV show of us walking the street.

So the quiet mind makes possible an overall awareness of the total situation, including ourselves. It's sometimes called an awareness of the Gestalt—in which separate elements of consciousness are so integrated that they function as a unity.

~

There's a guy up on the roof, right at the edge, with his infant son in his arms; he's threatening to throw him off and then jump himself. Homicide-suicide—happens a lot with children. He's been having trouble with his wife—mother interfering, they lock him out, he's sleeping in the hallway, and it's gone to the edge. That's where he is, and I'm up there with him. I'm the final guy in the hostage recovery system we set up in New York City, which I've been working in for eight years and heading up for the last two. We haven't lost anybody in all that time.

Now, if you're not able to see the whole picture—how he's reacting, where and who your backup forces are, what's on the street, how long it's been going on, your own past experience, the chance that this is a new kind, and certainly what's going on inside you from moment to moment—if you can't hold on to all of that and still be there listening to this guy in a way he can feel . . . chances are he's gonna go over the edge. Someone is going to be killed. We've learned that.

And he's in this very intense, complex public situation. Several of us are up there—a net in the street below, a lot going on all around. To say nothing of what's going on in him: this lack of self-esteem and manliness, feeling pushed around by his family, no work. But I also can recognize this overriding love he has for his child, who he's convinced would be better off dead than with those two. Sounds crazy, but it was real to him. So there's a lot for all of us to take in.

So I'm helping him get a sense, an awareness of everything that's happening, just so he has the picture of it all. And the more he does, the more he is opening up to me. Turns out what concerns him most is that there be a hearing at family court to work out fair custody. He wants a hearing. But he won't accept a promise from me, or a signed note. He tells us we got to get a lawyer and have it on legal paper—which we send out a car and find a local lawyer and get for him. When he feels he's got support from the system, he hands us the child. At that point we have to jump him, because we know that's the crucial moment to prevent the suicide. He gets pissed at me, because we were talking together and now this. And I have to give him this look of "That's how it all is, kid." Some part of him understands.

Other times, you're called into very tight situations which you have to loosen up. I was called into a classic family fight scene. A nine-by-twelve room with an eight-by-ten bed, on which is sitting a two-hundred-pound construction worker with a knife in one hand and the hair of his wife, who's half-naked on the floor, in the other. He's yelling about her infidelity, and he's already nicked her. Not much room to move around in. So in talking to him I'm trying to expand the situation. I try to get him to talk about how he got to this point, recognize he still has choices, and think about the future. It's like I'm making the room bigger, making more room for this guy. And I have to stay very steady to do that, because there is part of me which is saying, "Man, you got a lot of balls accusing your wife of something at a moment like this." But as soon as I could get him to pull back and look at it all, which is what I'm doing too, you understand, then there's a chance to see exactly what move will break through the pressure. That's how this one got resolved.

Funny thing is, I can't remember much of what I've been saying to people at the end of these episodes. I'm running very much on intuition from moment to moment. I've had special training, of course, but that becomes a part of you, and it's only a part of what you're calling on.

You have to be steady and quiet inside. You have to have a foundation of belief in the absolute value and beauty of life. You can't get too caught up in it all. You step back, get as much of the picture as possible, and you play it moment *to moment. That's what I've learned from hundreds of these situations.*

~

In the clarity of a quiet mind, there is room for all that is actually happening and whatever else might also be possible. Though we may be mindful of myriad details, our attention never wavers from the specific situation or person in need. The intimacy of our attention becomes a heart-to-heart lifeline made firm and fast; no one need fall from the edge. The quiet appreciation of the total situation and its inherent possibilities steadily moves things toward resolution; we find ways to step back. In a spirit of compassion and reverence for life, these various skills flourish and combine appropriately.

Such feats might seem to be the result of crisis. Many of us have experienced rising to the occasion under such conditions. The intensity of the situation keeps the mind from wandering. For most of us, fortunately or unfortunately, our helping work doesn't entail the intensity that brings forth these heightened faculties. But whatever the circumstances, and however extensive the training and experience, it's important to recognize that the faculties of awareness being called into play are exactly those we have been cultivating and discovering in the practice of meditation and the investigation of awareness. General laws are operating under particular circumstances.

Why, for example, if one was tightly attentive to a single object—a man on the edge of a roof—wouldn't everything else disappear from awareness? Because, as we've discovered, it is possible to notice a single thought, sensation, or situation arise, but not get totally lost in identifying with it. We observe the cloud but remain focused on the sky, see the leaf but hold in vision the river. We are that which is aware of the totality. And our skills develop with practice. First, we have to appreciate the value of such qualities of mind and desire to develop them. Next, we have to have faith in the possibility that we can indeed make progress. Finally, we have to explore and practice appropriate techniques. Twenty minutes a day of such practice can lead to results and the incentive to go deeper still. Continuous practice brings about great transformation of mind and leads to a new quality of service.

When we function from this place of spacious awareness rather than from our analytic mind, we are often surprised to find solutions to problems without our having "figured them out." It's as if out of the reservoir of our minds which contains everything we know and everything we are sensing at the moment, all that could be useful rises to the surface and presents itself for appropriate action. Sudden flashes of memory, past experience, or understanding seem to get expressed: "I can't explain it." "It just came to me." "It all suddenly became clear." "I forgot I even knew that."

We often call this quality of mind "intuition" but often we don't trust or honor it. Unlike our thinking mind, which arrives at solutions through a linear process of analysis which we can follow, the intuitive mind seems to leap to a solution. Perhaps the process is going on outside the range of our consciousness; perhaps we are delving into regions of the mind where thinking, in the conventional sense, is not necessary. Whatever, it is still an important resource of our minds and worthy of more than incidental attention.

~

My father was dying; my mother was panicking. They were three thousand miles away from me. I had a family and a job. And all the familiar questions of these experiences: when to be with them, when to be at home and at work; when to call, when to wait to be called; medical decisions; hospital or home; and simply what to say, how to be.

I'd think and think about all this, but I would reach a point where I'd see I had to stop. My mind would go "tilt." So I would go out and take a walk, or watch the river change tides and empty into the Atlantic. I'd watch kids at the playground. I'd see how the tree line had changed shape at the top of a mountain meadow I'd known for years. Things like that.

And sometimes I'd hear: "Right. It's time to be out there. I'll leave in two weeks and stay ten days." Or, "Not so much advice giving." Or "God is with them." The right thought. Something that would ring true. These seemed to come out of the blue, but I felt trust in them, and peaceful as a result.

It was very reliable and very inspiring, working that way. All through his illness and all the wild, anxious phone calls, I'd feel answers coming. It was very reassuring. I experienced it as grace. And at the end I was able to be with them at home and have his hand in mine as he died and my arm around my mother.

~

Ultimately, this kind of listening to the intuitive mind is a kind of surrender based on trust. It's playing it by ear, listening for the voice within. We trust that it's possible to hear into a greater *totality* which offers insight and guidance. Ultimately, but really ultimately, we trust that when we are fully quiet, aware, and attentive, boundaries created by the mind simply blur and dissolve, and we begin to merge into All That Is. And All That Is, by definition, includes answers as well as questions, solutions as well as dilemmas.

When we have been used to knowing where we stand at every moment, the experience of resting in awareness without any specific thoughts to hold onto and trusting our intuition, turns out to be a refreshing and exciting adventure. In this choiceless spacious awareness, we don't necessarily know from moment to moment how everything is going to come out. Nor do we have a clear idea of what is expected of us. Our stance is just one of listening . . . of fine tuning . . . trusting that all will become apparent at the proper time.

To rest in awareness also means to stand free of the prejudices of mind that come from identifying with cherished attitudes and opinions. We can listen without being busy planning, analyzing, theorizing . . . and especially judging. We can open into the moment fully in order to hear it all.

As we learn to listen with a quiet mind, there is so much we hear. Inside ourselves we can begin to hear that "still small voice within," as the Quakers call it, the voice of our intuitive heart which has so long been drowned out by the noisy thinking mind. We hear our skills and needs, our subtle intentionalities, our limits, our innate generosity.

In other people we hear what help they really require, what license they are actually giving us to help, what potential there is for change. We can hear their strengths and their pain. We hear what support is available, what obstacles must be reckoned with.

~

But he learned more from the river than Vasudeva could teach him. He learned from it continually. Above all, he learned from it how to listen with a still heart, with a waiting open soul, without passion, without desire, without judgment, without opinions.

Siddhartha, HERMANN HESSE

~

The more deeply we listen, the more we attune ourselves to the roots of suffering and the means to help alleviate it. It is through listening that wisdom, skill, and opportunity find form in an act that truly helps. But more than all these, the very act of listening can dissolve distance between us and others as well.

~

Heard... If they only understood how important it is that we be heard! I can take being in a nursing home. It's really all right, with a positive attitude. My daughter has her hands full, three kids and a job. She visits regularly. I understand.

But most people here... they just want to tell their story.

That's what they have to give, don't you see? And it's a precious thing to them. It's their life they want to give. You'd think people would understand what it means to us . . . to give our lives in a story.

So we listen to each other. Most of what goes on here is people listening to each other's stories. People who work here consider that to be . . . filling time. If they only knew. If they'd just take a minute to listen!

~

There are so many ways in which we listen to one another. "I hear you," we say to one another. Such a message would be welcome indeed if, for example, it came in the words of a trapped coal miner or a deaf person who had just undergone corrective ear surgery. In most helping situations, however, "I hear you" reflects a much deeper message: "I understand. I'm with you." Such a message can be immensely reassuring for a person who has felt isolated or alone in their pain and suffering. The reassurance does not come from the words themselves, of course, but from what the words represent. It comes if the person indeed *feels* heard.

It may not be that a particular story from one's life is so important. But sharing it is a way of being together— heart to heart. In those moments we are no longer alone with our fear; we are reminded that we are not forgotten.

> *When two people are at one*
> *in their inmost hearts,*
> *They shatter even the strength of*
> *iron or of bronze.*

How Can I Help?

And when two people understand each other
in their inmost hearts,
Their words are sweet and strong,
like the fragrance of orchids.

I Ching

To reach its full potential, however, this hearing from the heart requires that we remain alert to entrapments of the mind. Seeking to help others, we may start out open and receptive, but after a short time being with them seems to bring us down rather than lift them up. Somehow their suffering, self-pity, despair, fear, or neediness begins to get to us. It's a little like trying to pull someone out of quicksand and feeling ourself suddenly starting to sink. As reassuring as it may be for one depressed person to be heard by another depressed person, the relationship doesn't really open the door to escape from depression. Empathy is not enough.

Here, once again, our ability to remain alert to our own thoughts as they come and go serves us in our relations with others. We hear into their pain . . . they feel heard . . . we meet together inside the confusion. And yet we ourselves are able to note, perhaps even to *antici-pate,* that moment when another's entrapment of mind might be starting to suck us in. We are as alert to what is happening within *us* as we are to what is happening in *them.*

The ability to avoid being entrapped by one another's mind is one of the great gifts we can offer each other. With this compassionate and spacious awareness, and the listening it makes possible, we can offer those we are with a standing invitation to come out from wherever they are caught, if they are ready and wish to do so. It is as if we are in the room of experience with them, but also standing in the doorway, offering our hand, ready to walk out together.

~

A woman came to see me who was suffering greatly because of her daughter. She told me her daughter was real bad trouble. "She's run away to live with my other daughter down in Tennessee, and now she's forged a check with her sister's name on it, and she's gotten pregnant and she's only sixteen. I've been a seamstress all my life, supporting the kids and myself since my husband ran out when the youngest was still in the womb. Now she's run away, and you can't imagine what it's like. . . ."

I'm shortening the story. It actually took about fifteen minutes to run it all down. I just listened as openly as I could. I could feel her pain and discouragement and felt my heart hurt at the hard life she had had. At the same moment I felt very quiet inside, figuring maybe all I had to offer was to be with her. A little bit I felt she was wearing the albatross of this story, like the Ancient Mariner, and I was just another in a long line of people who had heard it. So when she finished I said, "Right."

She sensed I wasn't getting caught, and her immediate reaction was "No, you don't understand." And she recited the whole thing one more time, fifteen more minutes. And when she'd finished the second time, I said again, "Right."

This time she stopped for a moment. She'd heard me. She paused, and then said with a kind of wry smile, "You know, I was kind of a hellion when I was a kid, too." She just let it go.

~

For someone deeply trapped in a prison of thought, how good it can feel to meet a mind that hears, a heart that reassures. It's as if a listening mind is, in and of itself, an invitation to another mind to listen too. How much it can mean when we accept the invitation and hear the world anew.

~

When she first came to see me, this woman hadn't been speaking for three months. But she was silent in many different ways. Resentful silence: "You do it for me." Agitated silence: "I'm scared." Bored silence: "I have nothing." A kind of interested silence too—but not knowing how to start. After several months she began to speak.

Now, after a number of years, she spends a great deal of time talking, and she's afraid of silence, scared of being quiet. There are things, she says, that she doesn't want to know. Any movement into silence, from outside or within, is really frightening.

One day there was a noise outside. She paused and said, "What's that?" I said, "Let's listen." She listened for a moment and asked again, "What is it?" I said again, "Let's listen." And then she exclaimed, with total delight, "It's a bird! I haven't heard a bird in years. It's beautiful!" I saw it all go by: the noise; the not knowing (imagine the condition of one who doesn't know the sound of a bird!); her wish to hear; the listening; the sound recognized; the bird.

There was another long silence. Then she said, "That's just so beautiful."

~

The sage helps the ten thousand things
find their own nature.

Tao Te Ching

~

Much, then, can be accomplished in the work of compassion by exploring the activity of the mind. Through concentration, we are able to establish a more intimate contact with one another. Through spacious awareness we can sense the totality of situations and allow insight to come into play. More and more we are a vehicle for service. All of this may seem as if we are acquiring something new, but that is not so. Rather, we are clearing away obstacles that have prevented us from using our natural abilities. We regain what Suzuki Roshi, a Zen master, called "beginner's mind"—one that is open to the freshness of many possibilities.

To dissolve agitations and attachments of the mind is to remove the veils from our heart. It allows us to meet one another in the purity of love.

~

On the bulletin board in the front hall of the hospital where I work, there appeared an announcement. "Yeshi Dhonden," it read, "will make rounds at six o'clock on the morning of June 10." The particulars were then given, followed by a notation: "Yeshi Dhonden is Personal Physician to the

Dalai Lama." I am not so leathery a skeptic that I would knowingly ignore an emissary from the gods. Not only might such sangfroid be inimical to one's earthly well-being, it could take care of eternity as well. Thus, on the morning of June 10, I join the clutch of whitecoats waiting in the small conference room adjacent to the ward selected for the rounds. The air in the room is heavy with ill-concealed dubiety and suspicion of bamboozlement. At precisely six o'clock he materializes, a short, golden, barrelly man dressed in a sleeveless robe of saffron and maroon. His scalp is shaven, and the only visible hair is a scanty black line above each hooded eye.

He bows in greeting while his young interpreter makes the introduction. Yeshi Dhonden, we are told, will examine a patient selected by a member of the staff. The diagnosis is unknown to Yeshi Dhonden as it is to us. The examination of the patient will take place in our presence, after which we will reconvene in the conference room, where Yeshi Dhonden will discuss the case. We are further informed that for the past two hours Yeshi Dhonden has purified himself by bathing, fasting, and prayer. I, having breakfasted well, performed only the most desultory of ablutions, and given no thought at all to my soul, glance furtively at my fellows. Suddenly we seem a soiled, uncouth lot.

The patient had been awakened early and told that she was to be examined by a foreign doctor, and had been asked to produce a fresh specimen of urine, so when we enter her room, the woman shows no surprise. She has long ago taken on that mixture of compliance and resignation that is the facies of chronic illness. This was to be but another in an endless series of tests and examinations. Yeshi Dhonden steps to the bedside while the rest stand apart, *watching. For a long time he gazes at the woman, favoring no part of her body with his eyes, but seeming to fix his glance at a place just above her supine form. I, too, study her. No physical sign or obvious symptom gives a clue to the nature of her disease.*

At last he takes her hand, raising it in both of his own. Now he bends over the bed in a kind of crouching stance, his head drawn down into the collar of his robe. His eyes are closed as he feels for her pulse. In a moment he has found the spot, and for the next half-hour he remains thus, suspended above the patient like some exotic golden bird with folded wings, holding the pulse of the woman beneath his fingers, cradling her hand in his. All the power of the man seems to have been drawn down into this one purpose. It is palpation of the pulse raised to the state of ritual. From the foot of the bed, where I stand, it is as though he and the patient have entered a special place of isolation, of apartness, about which a vacancy hovers, and across which no violation is possible. After a moment the woman rests back upon her pillow. From time to time she raises her head to look at the strange figure above her, then sinks back once more. I cannot see their hands joined in a correspondence that is exclusive, intimate, his fingertips receiving the voice of her sick body through the rhythm and throb she offers at her wrist. All at once I am envious—not of him, not of Yeshi Dhonden for his gift of beauty and holiness, but of her. I want to be held like that, touched so, received. And I know that I, who have palpated a hundred thousand pulses, have not felt a single one.

At last Yeshi Dhonden straightens, gently places the woman's hand upon the bed, and steps back. The interpreter produces a small wooden bowl and two sticks. Yeshi

Dhonden pours a portion of the urine specimen into the bowl and proceeds to whip the liquid with two sticks. This he does for several minutes until a foam is raised. Then, bowing above the bowl, he inhales the odor three times. He sets down the bowl and turns to leave. All this while, he has not uttered a single word.

As he nears the door, the woman raises her head and calls out to him in a voice at once urgent and serene. "Thank you, doctor," she says, and touches with her other hand the place he had held on her wrist, as though to recapture something that had visited there. Yeshi Dhonden turns back for a moment to gaze at her, then steps into the corridor. Rounds are at an end.

We are seated once more in the conference room. Yeshi Dhonden speaks now for the first time, in soft Tibetan sounds that I have never heard before. He has barely begun when the young interpreter begins to translate, the two voices continuing in tandem—a bilingual fugue, the one chasing the other. It is like the chanting of monks. He speaks of winds coursing through the body of the woman, currents that break against barriers, eddying. These vortices are in her blood, he says. The last spendings of an imperfect heart. Between the chambers of the heart, long, long before she was born, a wind had come and blown open a deep gate that must never be opened. Through it charge the full waters of her river, as the mountain stream cascades in the springtime, battering, knocking loose the land, and flooding her breath. Thus he speaks, and now he is silent.

"May we now have the diagnosis?" a professor asks.

The host of these rounds, the man who knows, answers.

"Congenital heart disease," he says. "Interventricular septal defect, with resultant heart failure."

A gateway in the heart, I think. That must not be opened. Through it charge the full waters that flood her breath. So! Here then is the doctor listening to the sounds of the body to which the rest of us are deaf. He is more than doctor. He is priest.

I know ... I know ... the doctor to the gods is pure knowledge, pure healing. The doctor to man stumbles, must often wound; his patient must die, as must he.

Now and then it happens, as I make my own rounds, that I hear the sounds of his voice, like an ancient Buddhist prayer, its meaning long since forgotten, only the music remaining. Then a jubilation possesses me, and I feel myself touched by something divine.

~

5

Helping Prison

So many times each day we support each other informally without ever becoming "helper" or "helped." Perhaps we're finding an article of clothing for a partner, cutting bread for one of the children, collecting the mail for the person at the next desk, holding a coat for someone at a restaurant. But a situation defined is a situation confined. The moment the act requires a definition of the roles involved, we risk entrapment.

~

I'll give you a day in the life.

I work in this program with juvenile offenders, ex–drug addicts mostly. And I'm with this very tough, smart kid who tells me, "I got no time for programs, man. I seen programs." And I feel like saying, "Me neither. I'm not so crazy about programs myself." But here they are and there we were.

"Whadda you know?" he says. "You're just a social

worker. *Social workers are nowhere. Social workers don't understand shit."* And he's saying that a little angry and provocative. But it's a little wry, too. He was playing. And I was liking him at that moment, liking his style.

So I go, *"Yeah, all right. But that's all you think I am, a social worker? You don't see anybody here but a social worker?"* I was up for playing too.

"Well, you got a degree, right? They teach you about other people's troubles, right? That's how you got this job. You the Fixer, right?"

"Sure I got a diploma. I got a wife too. And I got a TV. And I'm into the Boston Celtics. If I'm just a social worker, maybe you're just an ex-junkie. Is that all that's happening here?"

Well, he sort of paused, and he heard it. And there was this moment where I felt something was about to get off the ground, like we were going to get past all this. It sort of hung there, one of those moments when you can feel possibility; maybe we can make it after all. And then . . . it was like we just missed. You could feel it get close and then pass by. And I swear he sensed that too.

He said, *"You got no idea where I am, man."* And I said, *"Well, you got no idea where I am."* He was being straight. I was being straight. Maybe we'd make it another time. Maybe we needed that honesty. But it was frustrating, because it got so close. I really liked this kid. Like, if we could have talked basketball . . .

So . . . bad day, or at least a frustrating one. Anyhow, I come home, lay back, and my wife comes in and tells me she's thinking about quitting her job at the hospital. I sort of half groan and half laugh. I'd been hoping *she'd* be the

one who'd have it together that evening. We take turns
being the one who has it together.

"Okay, what's the matter?"

"It's like prison in there. You've either got an ID badge
and a stethoscope or you're flat on your back helpless. It's
Us and Them, the sick and the healthy. The patients get
bugged, we get bugged, everybody gets bugged. I can't
stand the roles and the distances. It's not a hospital—it's a
prison!" And she's laughing a little, but it's a strong feeling.
And then she gives me this classic, exasperated line, again
laughing, "I don't want to be a nurse, I just want to help!"

So I say, "Poor kid . . ." and give her a hug, because it's
obviously been one of those days. And I say something like,
"Well, I don't want to be a social worker either. Social
workers don't understand shit. But what are we going to
do? Who's going to feed the cat? How do we get out of
jail?"

And we laughed, and had chicken, and talked, and made
love. And afterwards she said, "I'm still a little bit at the
hospital." And I said, "I know, I'm still a little bit with that
kid."

~

Obviously, it's often appropriate and harmless to meet in
roles in which one is helping and another is being helped.
People get sick, nurses nurse. Sinks get stopped up,
plumbers plumb. These are voluntary contracts between
those with immediate needs and others with relevant
skills. Were these to remain simply forms we enter into as
needed and then let go of lightly, all would be well. It's
the excess baggage we carry into these functional rela-

tionships that may end up confining us. "Helper" and "helped" become states of mind and ways to behave that go way beyond function. Entrapment in these alienates us from one another: a social worker and a juvenile offender just miss; a nurse and a patient seem worlds apart; a priest and a parishioner, so distant, so formal. What otherwise could be a profound and intimate relationship becomes ships passing in the night. In the effort to express compassion, we end up feeling estranged. It's distressing and puzzling.

If it's prison we're in, we righteous helpers, what are we charged with? Breaking and entering with the intention of doing good? Felonious assumption of personal responsibility? Selling water by the river? And what is our defense? Early conditioning? "They made me read *Helper Rabbit* every night until I was eight, Your Honor. In my house, the cry 'Help!' was an order, not a plea." Or later training? "I offer as Exhibit A, Your Honor, this diploma":

[Your name] has finally proved himself adequate in the eyes of the undersigned responsible parties, if not in his own. [Your name] is now okay. [Your name] has mastered certain rules for helping and promises to abide by them. [Your name] knows something others don't know. [Your name] has been trained in the use of a number of skills and had them licensed by the state. [Your name] will use them to make others whole. [Your name] is entitled henceforth to

call himself a D.C.P. (Doctor of Certain Powers). [Your name] may not immediately appreciate the predicament this will put him in or the constraints it may impose upon all. Best not to divulge too much, too soon. Which is why all this has been written in Latin.

~

All of us can recognize some truth to the plea of conditioning—first by our parents, then by our teachers. From earliest childhood many of us are told, "Be good and help." Helpfulness gets encouraged, often rewarded, because it makes the household function more efficiently. "Help out" becomes a euphemism for obedience or compliance.

Once we come to associate it with rewards, we start to use helping in the service of a wide range of personal motives other than the expression of natural compassion. We might empty the trash in order to get the use of the family car, or go to the store to fetch ingredients so that Mother will make our favorite cookies. We might be seeking to compensate for a lack of self-esteem, for feelings of unworthiness or incompleteness. Need praise? Help out. Or perhaps we're looking for a form of atonement: there's guilt to assuage. For many, the ability to aid others can provide a needed sense of power or respectability. Maybe some of us help out as a way of compensating for a deeper sense of helplessness; we don't have to face our own quite so much when we're busy treating someone else's. Or maybe we're just plain lonely. Intimacy is what we're looking for, and it's often there to be found in a helping relationship.

Rare indeed is the individual for whom the helping

act does not arise in part out of some personal motive. To the extent that it does, however, what we are looking for is a role that meets a need . . . our need. We're looking to be helpers, not simply to be helpful. A personal agenda leads us to invest in the position, not simply the function. And we invest in others' reactions to it as well.

~

I walk down the street, I'm nobody. Run for a bus, get in line at the store, punch in at work . . . who are you? Nobody special. And that's okay. Everybody's nobody most of the time.

But walk into that senior center—let me tell you, I'm somebody. "Hello, Mrs. Luchese. How ya been? They've been asking for you. Can you go see Mrs. Whoever; she had a fight with her daughter, that louse." I'm somebody. They say prayers for me, these people. My birthday . . . some lady—sure, she's a little screwy—she wants to make it a national holiday. I say, "That's a great idea. Me and George Washington." But I like that feeling. I need that feeling— that "somebody."

~

Often getting a few perks from our acts seems fine. But most of us can recognize moments when we get a little lost in such personal needs. In any relationship—marriage, friendship, work—there's that place in us which enjoys being the wise and compassionate one. We understand someone a little too quickly; or volunteer advice just too soon. Sometimes we have to be shown that all of us are better off when we're free of attachment to being helpers.

How Can I Help?

~

I happened to have been on a mountaintop in a state of great bliss when a stranger suddenly appeared next to me, sat down, and immediately started to describe this problem he was going through. By the time I'd pulled myself out of the Higher Realms, he'd already detailed the whole drama, the cast of characters, and the decisions he was facing. I hadn't gotten a bit of it. Nothing. Nobody. Moreover, it was much too late to ask him to run it all down once more. He would have felt very uncomfortable, justifiably.

So there I was, intimate confidant to a deep problem, without the slightest idea of who was who and who had done what to whom. My first reaction was to laugh hysterically. It was one of those great Human Condition moments. But this guy was obviously in distress and looking for a kindly pair of ears, so I picked up as best I could.

To my continued amazement, none of the details became any clearer as we walked down the mountain. I kept hoping I'd find out who "she" really was, and what "he" had actually done. No such luck. And I wasn't about to ask a question that would reveal my total ignorance, make him feel terrible, or lead me to hysterical laughter.

So we just quietly walked on down. And from time to time I would punctuate the conversation with what seemed like appropriate remarks: "That must have been hard." "What did you feel then?" "Oh, yes, I've been through that one before." "Boy, things sure do get confused in life." Great insights like that. And he would nod appreciatively, continue, and I'd contain my sense of this wonderful human absurdity. Meanwhile, I was growing increasingly fond of this guy. And feeling great empathy for his problem—whatever it was.

When we reached the bottom of the hill, he stopped for a moment and then suddenly embraced me. "I just want you to know how incredibly helpful you've been," he said. "You're one of the most understanding, compassionate people I've ever met. Do you think we could have another conversation like this again?" I was dumbfounded. It was one of the great moments in my life. "Sure," I said. "I'd love to." And he walked off to join some other people—a number of whom kept coming to me during the day saying, "What did you tell Eddie? He's just so grateful to you. He says you're wonderful."

~

The attachment to the role of helper is frequently reinforced by training that often contributes to a confusion between role and skill. Medical students in grand rounds, for example, get not only a direct view of pathology in patients but an equally intimate view of their teachers as role models. At the conclusion of a residency, a young doctor not only has mastered a complex body of knowledge but has learned how to play doctor as well. This medicine-man persona, while perhaps lending an aura that contributes to healing, also isolates the doctor from those around him.

But there is another dilemma of the diploma: help becomes know-how. Obviously training is valuable. We want our lawyers, counselors, and teachers to know what they're doing. Yet to identify them only with their know-how is to shortchange all and turn our relationship into a transaction between one who knows and one who doesn't. Patterns of behavior get frozen. The aura of know-how in the helper can undermine our confidence as the helped in defining issues for ourselves. We're a little unsure of the ground, don't know the technical language, generally uncomfortable. It must be our fault. Best we lie back and take what's given agreeably . . . and end up feeling still more helpless.

Identification of service with know-how has considerable occupational hazard for the helper as well. We begin to see people in categories. A psychiatrist treats "paranoid schizophrenics"; a lawyer meets with "litigious parties"; a politician woos "constituents"; a teacher works with "gifted" or "exceptional" children. To apply such discriminative models to people can be functional; to limit people to these does violence to their beings. Indeed, to view the world only in terms of concepts strips it of its mysterious beauty, its power to refresh.

So we are called upon to take what is valuable from our training, but not let it constrict the helping relationship itself. We need to enlist the service of the intellect, but not let it block the intuitive compassion of the heart. Not easy, this task. For the temptation to identify ourselves as What We Know is especially formidable when it comes to helping. We're moved by the desire to be of service in our lives. When useful know-how comes along that can help us satisfy that desire, it's not surprising that we embrace it, identify with it, feed it, go to conferences, read books about service (and write them!).

Once we have acquired all this knowledge, it's hard to keep it in perspective. It may dazzle us and make us forget the bedrock of wisdom to which all are privy. It gives us one kind of power but cuts us off from our birthright, the wisdom that comes directly from our common humanity and divinity.

Finally, when we identify with our special knowledge, we may develop a vested interest in being "right." In family life we need to prove our theories of child rearing. In professions we defend schools of thought. Helping often slips through the cracks.

~

I believe the real estate industry in this town is unwilling to provide affordable, adequate housing. And I think there are reasons why: property, profit motive, how capitalism works, and so on. I don't push this analysis at folks. But working as a tenant organizer, I'm looking for ways to get these points across to a large audience. It can get complicated.

I'd been working with a building where conditions were terrible. People there were becoming active—word of mouth in the hallway, some informal meetings, a few natural leaders coming forward—all this even though folks were a little uncertain of themselves and looking to me and my knowledge and experience.

Just about the time I was getting some interest from the press, one of the women who was showing some leadership—Carmen, a great lady—realized the time had come where we could push the landlord and get some repairs. He was sufficiently worried to make concessions.

Problem was, some part of me wanted to hold off. I wanted to wait for a greater confrontation. There was a chance for some publicity, a chance to make a larger point about housing in the city.

Carmen made her pitch at a meeting: "Let's go down there with certain demands, deal with this man, see what we can get. We're strong, we're ready." She ran it down very well. People looked to me: What did I think?

Now that's a key moment for an organizer. You're there to encourage people to move on their own, but you also have a commitment to a larger movement and a set of beliefs about how real change is going to come about. But when they were looking at me, I wasn't looking at myself.

I manipulated the meeting toward holding off confronting the landlord. I said we shouldn't sell out too early. I was going for my own agenda. I was persuasive, all the things you learn as an organizer, and I won them over. They'd hold off getting some immediate improvement in their lives.

As the meeting was breaking up, Carmen came up to me. She had this very won't-leap-to-conclusions-but-won't-take-any-bullshit look on her face. She said to me, very simply, "Are you being straight?" That's exactly how she put it. She was right on. She saw it. And she was giving me the chance to see it too. After a moment I said, "No, I'm not."

So I got people reassembled and told them I'd realized that I had been pushing my own interests and viewpoint rather than hearing theirs. I pointed out what it was like to be a tenant organizer with a theory of how to make change and build a larger movement. I said I thought they should talk it all over again and I should leave. I'd made what in my work was a bad mistake. They understood. They said, "We still need you," and I said, "I'll still be around." But they started discussing it all again.

As I left, Carmen gave me this great look. It was like a look of "Hmmmnnn. . . ." Curious, respectful, intrigued. It was as if she suddenly saw the whole issue of leadership, right at the moment she was becoming a leader. It was a great moment between us. Very encouraging.

~

Many times we may be alert to the risk of the role. Out of the corner of our eye we catch ourselves acting out our private agendas or see our attachment to certain self-images. But frequently the situation in which we're working tends to set traps. The dynamics may be subtle. People may need us to play helper. The service organizations so many of us work for have an investment in a collective self-image. Reputations, budgets, relationships in the community, need to be protected and promoted. By building and investing in formal helping institutions we often end up creating distances between who we think we are and those we'd like to serve. There may be some vague awareness of the problem, but in the end we rarely find "Attachment to Being a Helper" on the agendas of most staff meetings. Bring that issue up, the atmosphere in the room might turn a little cool. "Can we get on with business?" So little time, so much help needed.

Our conditioning, our motives, our training, our attachment to our ideas, the vested interest of organizations . . . all these, then, can seduce us into believing we've got the help, we are the "helpers." The self-image is very compelling. After all, we like to see ourselves as useful and compassionate. It feels good to be able to offer care to one another. We do have the talents and training to offer. But other factors, other needs are at work as well. We have a personal history to make sense of, a story line we're trying to write: "This Is Your Life." We need to present ourselves to others: "What do you do?" "Well, I'm a ———" and we've got to come up with some kind of answer, at least to ourselves. We've got to be somebody, after all. "Helper . . . yes, I'm a helper." That's a worthy identity.

Sad, then, that so often it imprisons us, that because of it we find ourselves accomplices to conditions of separateness and division—a world of nurses and patients, social workers and clients, spiritual teachers and seekers, people who know and people who don't. After all, if some of us are busy being helpers there must be others under continuous pressure to be helped.

The condition of helplessness is one that we tend to push away, deny, or stigmatize as a society and as individuals. Our cultural myths neither encourage us to accept a common helplessness nor teach us how to act upon it. When it's suddenly thrust upon us, we're unprepared.

For example, many of us feel resigned to helplessness as citizens. In a society that so inordinately emphasizes power, many of us feel we have little influence over conditions beyond our most immediate circumstances. We may see injustice and neglect or sense the sterility of mass culture. The quality of education, the organization of work, the anonymity of community life, all may distress us. But we frequently feel impotent to change these conditions. The choices we're given often seem empty and hollow. Half of us don't vote for president; even fewer elect local officials. We're offered thirty brands of blue jeans; everyone knows they're really the same. The program on television is a bore; we switch channels—some choice. Frustrations accumulate, resignation reigns. "What are we going to do?" we sigh. What's the point in dwelling upon it? It only makes us feel worse.

For those particularly weak and vulnerable, moreover, helplessness becomes a scarlet letter. The jobless steelworker loses self-esteem as well as income. The welfare recipient is at the mercy of bureaucracy and the seeming whim of a worn-out clerk. The senior citizen is haunted as much by the possibility of general helplessness as by any specific infirmity: to spend our last days in a nursing home, neglected and useless . . . ?

In many societies, however, the state of helplessness is so common that the experience has to be shared. There it is, after all—the poverty, the illness, the homelessness, the hunger, the death. It can't be denied or pushed to the back of the mind, because it's simply too prevalent. But as punishing as it can be, people also have a chance to see what strengths can emerge in its face. In the presence of helplessness they can also witness courage, perseverance, patience, acceptance, dignity, and humor.

Here, however, we shun helplessness, and when faced with it, bemoan our fate. We cling to notions of "independence"—it's the name of our national holiday—as if it were an essential condition of all well-being. The last thing we want is to be robbed of power and placed at the mercy of others. Under any circumstances that's a challenge. But in our society the most helpless among us are often consigned to a separate class: ghettos, "golden age" communities, hospitals, wards. They're *put* or *kept* somewhere. The rest of us are freer not to face what they represent.

Then, suddenly, something happens. We're struck by adversity—and a torrent of reactions. The shock at the loss of power: can't eat, can't wash, can't go to the bathroom alone; just this bell, and how long will it take for them to come this time? The shame: at having been raped and all these strangers know. The guilt: it was just a pleasant drive in the country, and suddenly a little boy is dead. The fear (My God, this is only the beginning!): the first chemotherapy treatment; the first day of torture in prison; the first day the bandages are off, and it's clear you're blind. And the helplessness: falling . . . falling . . . falling. . . .

~

It happened in a stroke. It was a stroke. And here I am, in a chair, half-paralyzed. And nobody and nothing prepared me for it, for the mind part of it.

Maybe there were chances and I missed them. Times I got sick, friends I might have visited in the hospital. But you do it for them, then you put it all out of your mind. Now I have no choice. I can't put it out of my mind. I'd do anything to avoid facing it.

~

Suddenly, the price of our conditioning becomes all too apparent. We've clung to models of ourselves as independent, defining ourselves largely in terms of our power to shape our own destiny. There's been little encouragement to acknowledge and explore our vulnerability. The weak, the afflicted, the vulnerable, the helpless—it's always been "them." Now, suddenly, we're "them."

Understandably, our tendency under such circumstances is to look for familiar ways to hold our ground. Behind false façades of courage or self-sufficiency our ego might seek to deny our helplessness. Since others support us in the effort, for a while this strategy keeps us going. But deeper down, there may be something evasive about it. We're calling upon old strengths, but are we facing the new situation? We're not quite sure who we are anymore. That's precisely what's so traumatic: our ego is adrift. For fear of not recognizing ourselves, we refuse to look into the mirror of the present moment.

Because our power is so threatened and our ability to control our environment so curtailed, we may explore ways of using our helplessness to gain power. Perhaps we get others to focus on our predicament. Controlling attention is power. Or perhaps we play on people's pity, guilt, or sense of duty. Instinctively, we seem to know that we can pull those strings. We remember, after all, how we ourselves used to feel in the presence of someone else's helplessness.

We become so busy trying to find old strengths or new devices to cope with our helplessness that we never really examine the condition itself. We may think we'll be giving up or giving in. And it's not surprising that we're not willing to let go altogether. The challenge is enormous. Not only must we deal with an affliction itself: we're being asked to confront our helplessness in the face of it. Can we imagine a more difficult task? At some level, we're being called upon to relinquish every model of ourselves that has kept us going until now—it's a leap into the void, with no ground to push off from. To enter into and explore our helplessness goes against every learned instinct—like turning a car wheel in the direction of a sudden skid.

Meanwhile, we're being "helped"—helped, that is, by

"helpers." And so often, as we've seen, the character of their work, colored by their own needs for power and self-image, only makes us feel still more alien and diminished. What they seem to want most from us is our compliance. They want us to be "helped." But that's not quite the same thing as inviting us, supportively, to explore our helplessness. This could be an obstacle to getting things done quickly and efficiently: "Don't dwell on such stuff." It threatens the ego; it's mysterious; it takes time.

Perhaps, despite all this, we might have a halting, tentative willingness to examine our helplessness. We might recognize that in the very midst of this upheaval there's a chance to confront our resistance and go beyond the perimeter of the familiar. With a little support we'd be ready to peer over the edge and look at our worst fears.

Still, conditions seem to conspire against it. The weight of circumstance, the accumulation of habits, the entrapment of roles are just too great. Reaching out, trying the best we can, looking for someone who recognizes our little effort, we just don't get the steady encouragement we need. Maybe there's one nurse, one friend, one phone call that gives us the courage to pursue this exploration further. But eventually we resign ourselves to joining the ranks of the "helped." As unhappy as we may be with this role, there seems to be no other option, no adequate support to find a new one.

Thus both helper and helped feel constrained. Both may experience the yearning to be free, may make attempts, may at times have small successes. But these often prove to be but short-duration furloughs. We find we're still doing time. It still feels like Helping Prison.

The philosopher Gurdjieff pointed out that if we wish to escape from prison, the first thing we must acknowledge is that we *are* in prison. Without that acknowledgment, no escape is possible. That is, as long as we feel that these roles are inevitable, functional, or the best we can do, it's unlikely that we'll be alert to alternatives.

Fortunately, many of us do recognize the entrapment of these roles. When we are able to step outside our situations for a moment and recognize the constrictions, we may even be prepared to acknowledge that somehow we ourselves are contributing to this sense of imprisonment.

There's great potential in that recognition alone. It's the beginning of our escape. Just to be alert to the entrapment can prevent it from taking complete hold without our conscious awareness. We're more on the lookout for ways to penetrate the walls: a loose brick here, a vent duct there. We find an opportunity and grasp it and suddenly begin to come out from behind the roles.

With that alertness we are ready to seize opportunities. A doctor comes in to ask how you are feeling, and you notice he's looking you in the eye; he's really asking. Now you can tell him how you *are* feeling . . . not just what your body is up to. An uncle who's been deeply depressed drops his guard and tells you just how much he misses his dead wife. The old family constraints fall away. He doesn't have to be strong, you don't have to be deferential. You can meet as friends, both of whom have known pain.

What's interesting when this happens is that we realize that the opportunity to meet behind the roles was present all along. It's a breakthrough to a state that was *there waiting*. Everyone breathes a sigh of relief because we feel that we are home again. It's not so much that we've solved a problem through technique, experience, or know-how. *We've simply remembered who we all really are behind the roles.* Of course, there's more going on than a one-dimensional transaction. After all, we're human beings here.

So we don't need devices or gimmicks to break through the walls of Helping Prison. Nor do we have to deny that we *can* help or we *need* help and that there are appropriate forms to give and receive it. What we can do, however, is allow ourselves to open to the fullness of our humanity. We can make room for it all. As we do this, *the richness and reciprocity of the helping act itself works to dissolve the barriers created by roles.*

It's clear, for example, that as helpers we don't simply go about dispensing service with nothing in return. We all know how much we get back from caring for others. Nor is it simply material reward, praise, or the feeling of having been useful. Something far more essential can be tapped.

~

You walk the halls of this place, and what do you see from room to room? Most people peer in and see this retarded child or that one. They focus on this particular mannerism or that deformity. I do it too. It's very compelling, that picture.

But one kid flipped me around on that. We were doing language exercises. And for some godforsaken reason I'd chosen the exchange "How are you?" . . . "I'm doing fine." We'd go back and forth. Well, he was having quite a hard time of it, slurring out, "Iy dluee fie" or some such. "Let's try again, really slowly," I said. "How . . . are . . . you?" And he slurred, "Iy dluee fie." Then he suddenly burst into this wonderful crazy slurry laugh. It was the nuttiest sound we'd ever heard, either of us. He wasn't doing fine at all. Neither was I. We were doing terribly. It was absurd. We just began to howl.

In the midst of that he suddenly gave me this very clear look—the eyes behind the expression. And I had a sudden thought: "My God, he knows more than I'll ever know about all this. He sees the whole situation." At which point he just scrunched up his face like a clown and gave me this wonderful wink.

I was just stunned. All I could see was this incredible sense of the humor of things. It was so deep in him. He just had it all in perspective. And he gave that perspective to me.

When I left him, my head was spinning. I walked down the hall and looked into the other rooms, at kids I'd known, or so I'd thought, for months. It was totally new. I don't quite know how to describe it. In this room I saw courage. In that room I saw joy. Across the hall, patience. In yet another room, such sweetness: a little boy who was so continuously filled with love, people would just—"die," I was going to say. "Live," really.

I felt so humbled. I swear I had the impulse to go down on my knees. Here I was, going around giving speech therapy, little lessons, little tips. And what was I receiving back in return? Humanity. Basic humanity. The deepest qualities of a person, deeper than you'd see most anywhere.

What a gift! How much it helped me in my work! In fact it really changed my life. How often can you say that?

~

When we see that service is not a one-way street, we find that those we are helping give us a continuous stream of clues to help us escape the prison of our self-image. More than simply letting us know what might be working or not, they help us when they question our very models of ourselves. They snap us to; they may even see right through us. And if we can take it, it's a blessing. We may feel a little foolish, but ultimately, we're grateful.

The struggles of those we are helping confront us with life at its purest. Their suffering strips away guile and leaves what is real and essential. The deepest human qualities come forth: openness, yearning, patience, courage, forbearance, faith, humor . . . living truth . . . living spirit. Moved and touched by these qualities, we've no choice but to acknowledge and reaffirm our humanity. Others notice when this happens. We feel them feel it. It's at these moments that we remember what service is truly all about.

~

She thanked me for helping. I thanked her for letting me. She said, "You helped me see who I really was." I said, "You showed me to begin with."

~

Our own experience with helplessness also points the way to escape from the prison of roles.

~

When I lost my vision, I had been very self-sufficient and together. I was raising five children. I was working. I was volunteering in my community. I was independent enough to be contemplating a divorce from a bad marriage—I'd even given an attorney five hundred dollars. Just before I had to go into the hospital.

I'd begun to find myself knocking things over and stumbling around. I went to an ophthalmologist, then a neurologist, then a radiologist, then a neurosurgeon. And finally a doctor said, "You have a growth in your brain. If you don't have surgery it will continue to grow and it will take your life." Just like that.

The operation took seven and a half hours. The doctor said he almost lost me twice. He'd removed a tumor the size of a hen's egg. All I could see was the faintest bit of light.

It didn't hit me until I got home. I didn't recognize myself. I went into the hospital with long hair; I came out with short. I went in at 145 pounds; I came out at 175, wearing my mother's dress. I went in and could see; I left and couldn't. It wasn't me. And things were bad at home. I couldn't get a divorce now; I was too dependent. I tried to do things for myself, but it often just created more trouble. My youngest daughter didn't want to be seen on the street with me. She was ashamed. I felt so bitter. But I kept pushing my feelings away. What had happened? Why me? I just wanted out of there.

How Can I Help?

One nice fall day, I told my husband I was going out. I went down the elevator and out of the house. I got to the corner and just stopped. I stood there, expecting any minute he'd come down and join me. He never came. I just stood there on the corner.

A lot happened on that corner. I saw my past life. I recalled how lonely and helpless I'd felt as a little girl. And there I was now, just like a child again, only with five of my own. I stayed there a long time. Finally, I said to myself, "Well, here you are and there's no place to go. It's time you brought a little help into your life."

So I went into rehabilitation. And I told them everything I felt. I gave them everything. I gave them my shame and my anger and my fear. I felt it was the truth. And if it was the truth, then how could I be helpless? You don't suffer from the truth. The truth sets you free.

Of course it was hard work, coming to terms with change. But after a while you have nothing left to hide. You want to bring it all out. You want to make room to receive help. And when you're with a lot of people who are also trying to do that, you get a lot of support. Us blind folks, working together: the more I felt that, the more I found myself beginning to offer help as much as ask for it.

I met a young man there who was blind from birth. He'd never had a birthday party. So I baked him a cake and organized a party. He blew out the candles he couldn't see. He was delirious. It was grand. I felt so happy. I had come from that lost blind person on the corner to someone who had seen a need and done something about it.

I've told people something that sounds a little cruel. Everyone should experience temporary blindness, to see how our vision can give us such hangups, how we judge and

condemn, and what that does to us all. *Like that boy with
the birthday cake. There was a blind girl he had fallen for.
Then someone said she was unattractive. He stopped seeing
her. It brought tears to my eyes. He'd been seeing fine.*

*But when you begin to see with that inner eye, that inner
eye everyone has, it all changes. Everyone is human, everyone is God's child. Everyone is helpless, one way or another,
and everyone is helpful too. We're all here for each other
. . . that's how it is. And we all have something to give, no
matter our condition.*

*There are ups and downs, of course. You start blind and
reach out. Sometimes there's nothing to hold on to, but you
still reach. Then you learn to hold on to whatever you get.
Then you find someone's hand and you take it. Then you
see you can reach out and hold someone else. Once you
start, it all follows. I've seen that.*

*So now, when I work with handicapped people, or any-
one really, I find I have a special understanding to share.
That's really all I have to offer. It's hard to put it into
words. It's just "I understand," that's all.*

*And yet, as sure or secure as that may sound, I don't
think you're ever really secure. What is security? You can
lose it in a flash. I know. And I still get shaky. So I have a
little prayer: that the Lord will send me someone to help me
along the way on my subway journey every day . . . and
that He'll send someone I can share my faith and strength
with too. Both things. That's how I set off to work. And it
usually happens.*

~

How special that moment when we stop pushing it all
away. Here is the moment of truth: the fear, the vulnera-

bility, the doubt, the helplessness—that's what's going on, that's what we're feeling. We're alone on a corner. But the moment we accept it, we're not running anymore. We've turned the corner and can finally say, "Now what?"

The minute we accept the place where we may seem helpless, it can cease to be the deepest truth about us. The part of us that's accepting it isn't the part of us that's lost in it. To regain that perspective is the beginning of freedom. Of course there is no assurance that we won't go under again . . . and again . . . and again. But something has changed. There is new buoyancy.

The process is painstaking, and for it to proceed we need great compassion for ourselves—exactly the way we are. And we must allow the universe to be exactly the way it is. Through this process we find that we are no longer pitting ourselves against things. We're opening to life—first by opening to ourselves, and then gradually expanding outwards.

As we explore our resistances and fears—everything we'd been so busy fighting before—new understanding and resources are revealed. Our old models of ourselves start to dissolve, leaving us open and receptive to the new moment. Now we can begin to work creatively with the unknown. We're ready to listen and accept guidance and grace, because we've made room in ourselves. We may be exhausted, yet at the same moment we feel fresh. Having surrendered into helplessness we can now get on with help.

But as active participants. Before, we had to be helped. Now, what we are ready for is *support,* for a process we have set in motion *ourselves.* So we reach out and receive it eagerly. It's become part of a dialogue with life, a dialogue in which we have things to say. We want to keep the conversation going. Help has become collaboration.

In this collaboration we see just how much we ourselves have to offer: our own perseverance, honesty, openness, gratitude, humor. And we may be amazed to find out how hungry people are for these qualities.

~

Sometime after turning the corner of my condition, I began to notice how conscious and thoughtful I was being with everyone around me. I was even a little embarrassed at all this new-found selflessness. But it felt so incredibly real and true and natural.

One doctor caught it. "I hear you've become the angel of mercy around here," he said. I said, "It's true." He laughed, "I understand." I said, "You're familiar with the process, doctor?" He laughed again, and I saw that he was.

"Does it last?" I asked, a little more seriously. And he laughed once more. "No. But it comes back. And you don't forget. And you appreciate being reminded."

~

And so at a certain point "helper" and "helped" simply begin to dissolve. What's real is the *helping*—the process in which we're all blessed, according to our needs and our place at the moment. How much we can get back in giving! How much we can offer in the way we receive! But even "giving" and "receiving" now seem artificial. Where does one begin, the other end? They seem to be happening simultaneously. That's how it feels, anyway. Isn't that why everyone's so pleased?

Now at last we're ready to play the roles—the final twist. Because at one level there *is* help to be offered and received. At one level there *are* forms. It's just that there are other levels as well. As we embrace them all—our helpfulness and our helplessness alike—we find ourselves able to enter into the forms without being entrapped by them. We can accept and thrive in the inevitable ambiguities and paradoxes.

The challenge, then, the opportunity really, is to accept the roles *in order to cut through them, and to cut through them in order to be able to participate in them without entrapment.* Once we taste the excitement of this process, we begin to recognize its profound implications. It's a chance to take on form in order to liberate one another from it. This is the true work of a conscious human birth. This is what we're all here to do.

So we enter into Helping Prison consciously. Here it is, after all. And it's fine, it's fascinating. In fact, Helping Prison is just where we might want to start out if liberation happens to be our goal.

~

You have to go through seven gates to get to where I work: "Solitary," known here in prison as "Special Housing," a.k.a. "the Box." I run education projects, and keep my eyes out for anything else.

By the time I've passed through the gates, I've seen hundreds of people. "Cómo estás?" "Yo, suckah!" "Hey, what's happening?" And there's an incredible gallery in here. (That's what they call cell blocks—galleries.) And a constant game of Who's Who. I see it at various levels.

Inmates are here, for starters, because they've either committed or been close to certain crimes. I also see that the system has produced conditions that make it pretty easy for that to happen. But they've made decisions too. So you've got the one of circumstance and choice weaving back and forth. And, of course, everyone has their story, and all that's part of it too.

It's just as complex with the guards. They're jailers, but they're also fellow employees of mine. And they're stuck in regular routines like the prisoners, stuck having to be "the Man." But they're choosing that too. And they're a little suspicious with me. Are prisoners going to put one over on this guy? That's okay, but sometimes it's delicate.

Recently I had two guards around me coming on with "Whadda we gonna do with these Commie teachers?" "I don't know. I'd like to find them buried under ten feet of snow in the spring." "You one of these new Commie teachers?" "No, man," I said. "I'm an anarchist. I got nothing to do with Commies."

It was a hard moment, actually. I saw a real deep hurting kind of suspicion about people like me, brought in here to give inmates education, while they can't afford to send their sons to college or get them a job in the area, except in this lousy joint.

So it's pretty complicated. The guards are watching out for anything that's going to make life difficult. The inmates are looking for whatever's going to make it easier. These guys are over here, those guys are over there, and I'm coming up the middle. So it's got to be Something For Everybody. Because you can't help somebody out if someone else thinks they're losing because of it.

So my approach is "Let's see if we can all shake loose a little and not get too lost in it and see what we can do." And I'm constantly looking for clues, clues to why we're all here, clues to what's possible. My bias generally is for a kind of harmonization, seeing it all like a chord that's trying to be resolved. I also have to do it because I can't afford to mess up. Very tense situation, the Box.

Thirty-two very heavy people—contraband, drugs, violent acts, political prisoners, guys who get raped, guys who rape them. And very close, everybody on the edge, waiting, rapping; everything reverberates.

Meanwhile, here I am, rolling up and down the corridor of the Box on my little office chair, from cell to cell, with books and magazines. Quite a sight, I'm told. And I'll open up an inmate's food hatch, peer in, establish contact, and see what kind of program we can get going. I'm on my rolling chair. He's on his plastic pail, a little puzzled. The guards are glowering, anywhere from suspicious to hostile. I may have a good chair, but I'm afraid.

But what I seem to be doing here seems to be needed. And what I seem to be doing here is also whatever I must have been curious about to get this job in the first place. It's a need, I think, simply to explore. What is all of this imprisonment and violence and separation all about, anyway? I'm trying to explore that in myself—the everyday fear and anger in my own life.

That's my education program in the Box. Are there any answers to this incredible human dilemma? Can we get into some kind of larger, greater conversation where we're just telling each other, "Look, this is what it feels like to be me going through this, and you tell me what it feels like to be you." And we'll try to do that with a certain kind of basic decency and sanity. That seems to me the beginning of freedom—something very much on people's minds here, everywhere really.

It happens. One day I'm squatting by one of the cells with a kid who is bending my ear off. Angel Cruz. "Hey, mister, thanks for coming by, I gotta list of books, I got me a plan I got to tell you about." Live wire. He'd been looking at this issue of *Solar Age* magazine. And he's no hippie Whole Earth domehead. He's just into solar cells, not prison cells.

"With one of these, I could move to Alaska, man. Get away from all this shit, grow my own vegetables, cheap electricity, and set up." And I'm right there with him—the thought of moving to Alaska having occurred to me from time to time.

"Okay, Angel. Where do you start?"

"Well, finish up clean here, get me some plans from this other book, do me some more research. . . ."

And we're really into it, back and forth, when all of a sudden, down the hall, here comes Mayhem. Yelling, screaming, the Goon Squad coming in in special uniforms. Possible riot, chance to spread. But Angel Cruz and I aren't dropping one stitch in our conversation. Angel Cruz and I are talking Serious Alaska here in the midst of this storm. And there's some kind of sanctification in it. It's a place of consecration which we two are keeping going together, both very aware that the stakes of keeping the conversation alive are somehow very high. And we're doing it.

I can't tell you how much that conversation meant. It was so important. Everyone is flipping out. But I'm with

Angel at the heart of his dreams, and Angel's with me at the center of my fear. And we're out of jail. We're building a solar hut in Alaska.

So you might say, "Who's helping who?" We're just two guys talking freedom. And yeah, we've got these different situations. But we don't have to get so locked into the Box that we can't go to Alaska together. And that's helping relieve me of my biggest burden in life: the feeling that I'm responsible, that I gotta do it. Responsible for this place, and my family, and friends. That's probably what brought me to the Box in the first place. That's what I'm doing time for—three counts of taking things personally. Personal responsibility, heavy felony!

So there's a great deal of to-and-fro in here. I'm telling guys about this, and they're telling me about that. And they're giving me advice about my life, and how it all is. Sometimes it's germane, and sometimes it's not. But it's frequently very funny, and I love it. I love moving in and out. I love the whole conversation.

~

6
The Way of
Social Action

In the middle of the gentle Indian night, an intruder burst through the bamboo door of the simple adobe hut. He was a government vaccinator, under orders to break resistance against smallpox vaccination. Lakshmi Singh awoke screaming and scrambled to hide herself. Her husband leaped out of bed, grabbed an ax, and chased the intruder into the courtyard.

Outside, a squad of doctors and policemen quickly overpowered Mohan Singh. The instant he was pinned to the ground, a second vaccinator jabbed smallpox vaccine into his arm.

Mohan Singh, a wiry 40-year-old leader of the Ho tribe, squirmed away from the needle, causing the vaccination site to bleed. The government team held him until they had injected enough vaccine; then they seized his wife. Pausing only to suck out some vaccine, Mohan Singh pulled a bamboo pole from the roof and attacked the strangers holding his wife.

When two policemen rebuffed him, the rest of the team

overpowered the entire family and vaccinated each in turn. Lakshmi Singh bit deep into one doctor's hand, but to no avail.

When it was over, our vaccination team gathered in the small courtyard. Mohan Singh and his exhausted family stood by the broken door of their house. We faced each other silently across a cultural barrier, neither side knowing what to do next. Such an event—a night raid and forcible smallpox vaccination—was unprecedented.

Mohan Singh surveyed his disordered household, and reflected. For a moment or two he hesitated. Then he strode to his small vegetable plot and stooped to pluck the single ripe cucumber left on the vine. Following the hospitality creed of his tribe, he walked over to the puzzled young Indian doctor whom his wife had bitten and handed him the cucumber.

I had stood in the shadows trying to fathom the meaning of this strange encounter. Now I reached out to Zafar Hussain, a Muslim paramedical assistant assigned to me by the Indian government as guide and translator. What on earth was the cucumber for? Speaking in Hindi, Zafar passed my question along to one of the vaccinators, a Westernized Ho youth, who challenged Mohan Singh in the staccato rhythm of the tonal Ho language.

With great dignity, Mohan Singh stood ramrod straight. The whole village was awake now, people standing around the courtyard stage as the rising sun illuminated our unfolding drama. Measuring his words carefully, Mohan Singh began:

"My dharma [religious duty] is to surrender to God's will. Only God can decide who gets sickness and who does not. It is my duty to resist your interference with his will.

We must resist your needles. We would die resisting if that is necessary. My family and I have not yielded. We have done our duty. We can be proud of being firm in our faith. It is not a sin to be overpowered by so many strangers in the middle of the night.

"Daily you have come and told me it is your dharma to prevent this disease with your needles. We have sent you away. Tonight you have used force. You say you act in accordance with your duty. I have acted in accordance with mine. It is over. God will decide.

"Now I find you are guests in my house. It is my duty to feed guests. I have little to offer at this time. Except this cucumber."

I felt numb and torn. For an instant, I wondered if I was on the wrong side. Mohan Singh was so firm in his faith, yet there was not a trace of anger in his words. I scanned my teammates' faces, looking for someone to respond to Mohan Singh's challenge. All stared at the ground, humbled by the power of Mohan Singh's faith.

~

I have spent twenty-five years struggling against racism. Worked in the South, worked in the North, saw people beaten, saw people killed, won a few, lost a few. I've yelled and I've screamed, and I've stopped and I've prayed. And I've wrestled with one basic question all along. Can the *spirit* of social action bring about change? Not just what we do, but the way we do it.

~

The problem of social action raises a number of unique challenges. In our own personal lives, we may work to remember who we truly are, to open our hearts and quiet our minds, and to see through the illusion of entrapping roles and forms. When that's really happening, we experience unity, suffering is eased, and all are nourished. For many of us, however, the instinct to help out finds expression in political initiative—so much of which seems based on opposition, not unity. It means encountering profound differences of belief, challenging institutions, struggling for power, risking casualties. How do we stay clear and conscious in the midst of all that? How do we maintain the integrity of Spirit on the battlefield of social action?

"I will not fight," says Arjuna, the hero in the Bhagavad Gita, as he surveys the battlefield and sees in the opposing army his cousins, friends, teachers: members of the human family all. The prospect of battle (generally a metaphor for struggle in human action) is too much; Arjuna throws down his sword. Yet Krishna (the voice of higher wisdom, God incarnate as Arjuna's charioteer) calls on him to face the world of conflict and confrontation. "Prepare for war with peace in thy soul," he counsels.

Tall order. We're asked to enter into this volatile environment of division and separateness, but with as much consciousness of unity as possible. So King sets out for Selma. Gandhi begins the Salt March. Or any number of us join movements for peace and justice. Seeking to recruit others, experiencing divisions among ourselves, confronting opposing powers, wrestling with fear and anger, trying to keep a clear sense of our goals . . . there are plenty of places to get lost in the struggle. We need all the clarity and inspiration we can get in order not to violate, in our own behavior, the very principles and ideals we're fighting for.

We look around, see injustice, oppression, the threat of war, war itself, and something inside grabs us: we've got to do something, it's time to act. But what is the spirit of that resolve? The initial state of mind we bring to any social action can go a long way to determining its character and consequences, especially if we're looking to move others to act.

~

I'll stand up at a meeting of people who are a little unsure of how they feel about the nuclear issue, and I'll see this basic, initial question in their faces even before I say a word: "Where's this guy coming from?" It's very instinctive, and very smart. People understand: First things first. So how do you come in? Do you come in, or do you come on? No small matter.

~

There's one thing I've learned in twenty-five years or so of political organizing: People don't like to be "should" upon. They'd rather discover than be told.

~

Sometimes it's enough just to share information with others: the number of nuclear warheads deployed and poised; the wage rates of women compared to men; the unemployment statistics for minorities; how many children starve to death in a single day. We trust these situations to speak for themselves. Injustice will strike others as injustice has struck us. We're appealing to collective understanding and compassion. It's Us talking it all over, seeing what We need to do.

But much of the time we come into social action—knocking on a door with a petition, addressing a meeting, writing a pamphlet, showing up at a demonstration, or just talking informally—and we're just a little self-righteous. We're convinced we've got something to say, something we're "correct" about. We've got our ideology and our scenario: here's how the situation really is, and the facts to back it up, if you'd take the time to read them, and if we all don't do this there's going to be that, so you better get started, and right away, right now.

Some of the time this attitude is blatant; at other times it's more understated. But at some level what we're communicating is the feeling that *we know*, others don't, and we've got to Change Minds. Changing Minds is a tricky game, especially when it's being fed with urgency and self-righteousness. There's often an air of superiority in what we say. People instinctively back off. They feel like they're being told, being "should" upon. Social action, they understand intuitively, ought to be fully voluntary if it's to have power and endurance. But we're not quite leaving them enough room when we set about trying to change their minds. We don't have the inclusiveness, the steadiness, the real willingness to listen that is critical at the outset of any action. It's not quite Us—it's this one trying to move that one.

In that environment, concerned as we are with results, we call on tactics of persuasion, appealing to states of mind that get people going. We begin to manipulate consciousness. Play to anger. Go for fear. There's always guilt. These basic states of mind are always lurking about, looking to be fed. They find plenty of nourishment in the world of social action: anger at oppression, guilt at being "better off," fear of violence and the greater power of others. They make a good case for themselves, pointing to all the provocation and evidence right here at hand.

Sometimes these feelings get us going—just the kick in the pants we may need. And we can keep them in check, in fact work with them. We can turn anger at injustice into cool, steady resolve. We can flip fear of war into greater reverence for life. We can find in feelings of guilt a call to greater moral sensitivity and alertness.

Yet left to themselves, fear, anger, and guilt are unwholesome states of mind. *How many of us have them fully in control in our private lives?* They pull us into a cycle of reactivity and feed on themselves. We begin to lose sight of the conditions that might have provoked them in the first place. In addition, they tend to be addictive and toxic. History is filled with examples of how these attitudes, which initially may have stirred people to action, went on to poison and destroy well-intentioned movements for social change. These are powerful states of mind we're playing with. Intentionally set in motion, their effect is usually incendiary.

Moreover, these states of mind blur our judgment and blind us to tactics that might be more reliable sources of action. Caught up in these emotions, we lose our timing and make mistakes. Our hearts grow cold; we turn people off. We're too worked up to hear our own inner voice, let alone trust anyone else's. What benefit in that?

They also prevent us from calling upon deeper human virtues that often move us all to act. In anger, we may lose sight of love. In fear, we may sacrifice trust and courage. In guilt, we may deny self-worth and obstruct inspiration. Do we really want to lose access to all these? If we really care about social change, can we afford to sacrifice such sources of commitment and strength? Are we serious or not?

We need to explore ways to reach one another and get started that don't set us off on the wrong foot. The handbill that announces the first meeting of a local parents group ... the fund-raising letter that seeks support for famine relief ... the mood of the crowd as it awaits the outset of the march ... the way you phrase a question to a city councilwoman who's a little astonished at all these people who've shown up at her office ... these aren't incidental moments or trivial matters of presentation or public relations. We're communicating the spirit behind the initiative. That's usually the message people react to first of all, if not most of all. *What spirit will it be?* How will we come forward? We can share information and conviction: here's our passion, our sense of urgency. But if "people don't like to be should upon, they'd rather discover than be told," then our invitation will probably be most effective when it communicates trust and respect. And honesty as well: We have to stay conscious of the ways in which our own lives still lack integrity and consistency. We're strongest when we act from what we have in common. We usually have to listen for that before we can really begin to act. Even the slightest bit of self-right-eousness can get in the way.

~

We were standing at attention, just a bunch of ordinary guys called up for this situation: a major demonstration in Washington against the war in Vietnam. Our job was to protect the Pentagon, which was a ludicrous idea to most of us—about as ludicrous but not as funny as this group of people over to a side who were doing this magical ritual in which they were going to levitate the Pentagon. They had chants and dances and they were into it and having a great time. I liked it. One guy actually yelled, "I saw it rise, I swear." It was hard not to laugh, even feel a part of it. I was rooting for it to rise too—why not? But I couldn't really be a part of it, at least at that moment. And it wasn't any easier because of how the rest of the demonstrators were treating us.

Anyhow, this girl approached me and placed this flower in my rifle. She didn't even look me in the eye. I might have been anyone. Then she stepped back, and everyone applauded and congratulated her, and she looked pretty pleased with herself. And they had this "Make Love, Not War" poster, but it didn't feel like love to me. It was like I wasn't even there. But of course I was. Turned out there was a picture to prove it. Right on the front page of the paper, with me standing there looking like a stiff and her all angelic. The Associated Press got hold of it and it went out all over the world. I felt used. Thing is, I'd been coming around to feeling the war was wrong. But that experience just pushed me back. There was nothing among those peo-

ple in front of me that felt like they were inviting me in. If anything, quite the contrary.

So I stayed kind of noncommittal for a while afterwards. A year or so later, I went down to Fort Benning to visit two Army friends who were getting ready to ship out to Vietnam. We hung out at this coffeehouse near the base. Very interesting place. New records, magazines, nice feeling, you could smoke a little out back, and just relax and talk among soldiers away from the base. I found out it was run by some antiwar activists, who had been setting them up at bases all around the country. Very simple idea. Just right. I talked to the guy who ran this one. He said, "Well, these guys are going to be doing the fighting. . . ."

So there was an atmosphere of frank talk among the soldiers. And I heard how most of them really questioned the war, how low morale was out there, how guys were basically ducking and staying low. One guy said, "You know where the real peace movement is? In the foxholes. The guys who are just keeping alive and not diving into this whole mess. That's what's going to end this war." And it's true. It's still an unwritten story about Vietnam. That night, at that coffeehouse, was the moment I really decided to become active against the war.

I did some work with Vietnam Vets Against the War. That was when I went back to Washington for the first time since that demonstration when I was in the Guard. We went there to meet with congressmen and other officials and to establish this outside encampment which would be there as a statement in itself. It was quite something for guys to be huddled around fires again, only this time right at the foot of the U.S. Capitol.

For me it was ironic too, because the last time I had been

guarding the government, and this time I was talking to it. "Sir, here's what's going on out there...." And they listened. They had to. These were the guys who'd been there. And if the men aren't really behind it, and they're taking all kinds of drugs, and even potshots at officers, which was happening ... well, they paid attention to us all right, and we just let the story speak for itself.

If people wanted to come by the encampment, we'd talk to them. If the media wanted to come by, we'd talk to them. The camp was a free zone for whoever showed up. And that was a powerful message: an army encampment open to all. I can't tell you what the net effect of it was. Who knows? I will say this: Everyone I met seemed deeply moved by something about it. I felt we had real strength and power and self-respect and other people's respect. There was truth in it. And I could see all that in the eyes of the officials. They recognize power when they see it. So we were a strong force just by our presence there.

Before leaving Washington I went over to where that demonstration at the Pentagon had been, several years before. I could see the whole episode like a movie ... including that flower child. I didn't have any bad feelings about her. She was just playing her part. The Pentagon still looked pretty solid, however. We haven't levitated it yet, although I definitely think we should go on trying.

~

A coffeehouse. An encampment. A free zone for whoever shows up. We're an environment, not an argument for social change. Our aim is to awaken together and see what follows, not to manipulate one another into this action or that.

We do so by recognizing the integrity of one another's experience. "What have *you* been through? What did it look like to *you*?" The most effective political action often grows out of telling one another our stories. We're out to share not to convince; action follows. So two policemen, talking off-duty, discover they both feel uncomfortable with racist jokes at the station; they agree to call people on them from now on. A group of women employees, chatting at lunch, find out they've all been sexually harassed by men with power over their jobs; they'll raise the issue at the next union meeting. Parallels of private experience become the ground for common initiative. What's been dealt with in solitude becomes the basis for solidarity.

It's a politics of affinity. We don't try to deny or manipulate individual differences. We honor them; in fact we seek them out—because we understand that before we undertake any serious social action, we need a strong sense of who we are. We have to move toward an initial state of unity, openly arrived at. The process can be painstaking. Decisions get delayed as we hear each other out and wait for consensus. Interminable dialogue . . . acting out . . . repetitions . . . boredom! And the time finally comes when what needs to be said (and we hope we hear it together) is "Enough already! How do we move? When do we act?"

Respecting one another's freedom, listening into one another as we initiate action, is a demanding task. It forces us to stay in touch with principles we've come together to fight for in the first place. Peace? Compassion? Concord? Are these qualities among us here and now?

The basic social institution is the individual human

heart. It is the source of the energy from which all social action derives its power and purpose. The more we honor the integrity of that source, the more chance our actions have of reaching and stirring others. But we must be *whole*-hearted, fully integrated as we set out. If we are not rooted in compassion, how will our acts contribute to a compassionate world? If we cannot move beyond inner discord, how can we help find a way to social harmony? If we ourselves cannot know peace, *be* peaceful, how will our acts disarm hatred and violence? "There is no way to peace," said A. J. Muste. "Peace *is* the way."

None of this means that we turn away from *what is:* oppression, hatred, fear. We have to look at it all head-on, without fantasy, denial, or selective perception: the brutal as well as the gentle, the ugly as well as the beautiful, the greed as well as the mercy, the death as well as the life. This takes guts, and judgment. But it can be the source of equanimity because we've pushed nothing away. We're ready to take it *all* in and then move beyond it. So we can let our hearts be broken by the spectacle of cruelty and allow our anger to arise at the evidence of injustice. Yet we can be whole and expansive enough to retain a sense of compassion and quiet determination—a fuller heart, a deeper will. Others—those we would encourage to join us in action—will recognize in us the possibility of unifying genuine passion and quiet purpose.

When the time comes to get started, then, we'll communicate a real sense of readiness. Our power will come forth from who we all are and know ourselves to be. It will be communicated in the quality of our presence, not just the substance of our message. We don't have to announce it. We will just show up—like the former warriors encamped at the seat of government to protest the government's war. We don't have to force our convictions; people reach out to hear them. But whatever the reaction, we have endurance to persevere in our efforts, because the spirit of our action has been sound from the start.

It's also critical to establish this more centered foundation for social action because conflicts are inevitably going to arise as we press our case, some anticipated, others unexpected. How, for example, will the cop who's heard enough racist jokes call attention to the next one without provoking still more anger: "What are you, my judge?" How will the women office employees who make it clear that there's been enough sexual harassment on the job deal with men's likely effort to demean them: "Why are you so uptight? Can't you take a little flirting?" When we're free of self-righteousness, grounded in a kind of inner clarity and quiet self-assurance, we're less likely to rush in simply to prove our point—only to contribute to a chain of reactiveness in which the issue gets lost and the polarization makes it harder even to start over again. We just don't get sucked in.

We may have to wait and let those we're confronting run through all their reactions. We *are* putting them up against themselves and their habits, after all. It *is* a little unexpected; sure, they feel they're on the spot. But the point is not to force any change of heart; hearts usually don't change under external pressure. What we're doing, at least at this stage, is giving people a chance to hear for themselves. We're looking to win a little space for our message to work on its own. So their reactiveness needn't throw us. In fact, it gives us a chance to demonstrate that we ourselves are ready to listen. Conflict isn't an obstacle. It's an opportunity to move forward. You don't push against it; you move to work with it.

As we take this attitude into the arena of social action, we're preparing ourselves for the inevitable unexpected. Quieter, more assured, more *interested* in how the process is unfolding, we're better able to size up new situations and sense when it's better to lie back and when best to step forward. We can begin to hear what's behind the struggles we encounter. We're more skillful tacticians, nimbler, on our toes, ready for conflict if necessary, but always alert to possibilities for reconciliation—not just an end to conflict but a greater harmony than when it all began.

~

The train clanked and rattled through the suburbs of Tokyo on a drowsy spring afternoon. Our car was comparatively empty—a few housewives with their kids in tow, some old folks going shopping. I gazed absently at the drab houses and dusty hedgerows.

At one station the doors opened, and suddenly the afternoon quiet was shattered by a man bellowing violent, incomprehensible curses. The man staggered into our car. He wore laborer's clothing, and he was big, drunk, and dirty. Screaming, he swung at a woman holding a baby. The blow sent her spinning into the laps of an elderly couple. It was a miracle that the baby was unharmed.

Terrified, the couple jumped up and scrambled toward the other end of the car. The laborer aimed a kick at the re-

treating back of the old woman but missed as she scuttled to safety. This so enraged the drunk that he grabbed the metal pole in the center of the car and tried to wrench it out of its stanchion. I could see that one of his hands was cut and bleeding. The train lurched ahead, the passengers frozen with fear. I stood up.

I was young then, some twenty years ago, and in pretty good shape. I'd been putting in a solid eight hours of Aikido training nearly every day for the past three years. I liked to throw and grapple. I thought I was tough. The trouble was, my martial skill was untested in actual combat. As students of Aikido, we were not allowed to fight.

"Aikido," my teacher had said again and again, "is the art of reconciliation. Whoever has the mind to fight has broken his connection with the universe. If you try to dominate people, you are already defeated. We study how to resolve conflict, not how to start it."

I listened to his words. I tried hard. I even went so far as to cross the street to avoid the *chimpira*, the pinball punks who lounged around the train stations. My forbearance exalted me. I felt both tough and holy. In my heart, however, I wanted an absolutely legitimate opportunity whereby I might save the innocent by destroying the guilty.

"This is it!" I said to myself as I got to my feet. "People are in danger. If I don't do something fast, somebody will probably get hurt."

Seeing me stand up, the drunk recognized a chance to focus his rage. "Aha!" he roared. "A foreigner! You need a lesson in Japanese manners!"

I held on lightly to the commuter strap overhead and gave him a slow look of disgust and dismissal. I planned to take this turkey apart, but he had to make the first move. I wanted him mad, so I pursed my lips and blew him an insolent kiss.

"All right!" he hollered. "You're gonna get a lesson." He gathered himself for a rush at me.

A fraction of a second before he could move, someone shouted "Hey!" It was earsplitting. I remember the strangely joyous, lilting quality of it—as though you and a friend had been searching diligently for something, and he had suddenly stumbled upon it. "Hey!"

I wheeled to my left; the drunk spun to his right. We both stared down at a little, old Japanese man. He must have been well into his seventies, this tiny gentleman, sitting there immaculate in his kimono. He took no notice of me, but beamed delightedly at the laborer, as though he had a most important, most welcome secret to share.

"C'mere," the old man said in an easy vernacular, beckoning to the drunk. "C'mere and talk with me." He waved his hand lightly.

The big man followed, as if on a string. He planted his feet belligerently in front of the old gentleman, and roared above the clacking wheels, "Why the hell should I talk to you?" The drunk now had his back to me. If his elbow moved so much as a millimeter, I'd drop him in his socks.

The old man continued to beam at the laborer. "What'cha been drinkin'?" he asked, his eyes sparkling with interest. "I been drinkin' sake," the laborer bellowed back, "and it's none of your business!" Flecks of spittle spattered the old man.

"Oh, that's wonderful," the old man said, "absolutely wonderful! You see, I love sake too. Every night, me and my wife (she's seventy-six, you know), we warm up a little bottle of sake and take it out into the garden, and we sit on an old wooden bench. We watch the sun go down, and we look to see how our persimmon tree is doing. My great-grandfather planted that tree, and we worry about whether it will recover from those ice storms we had last winter. Our tree has done better than I expected, though, especially when you consider the poor quality of the soil. It is gratifying to watch when we take our sake and go out to enjoy the evening—even when it rains!" He looked up at the laborer, eyes twinkling.

As he struggled to follow the old man's conversation, the drunk's face began to soften. His fists slowly unclenched. "Yeah," he said. "I love persimmons, too. . . ." His voice trailed off.

"Yes," said the old man, smiling, "and I'm sure you have a wonderful wife."

"No," replied the laborer. "My wife died." Very gently, swaying with the motion of the train, the big man began to sob. "I don't got no *wife*, I don't got no *home*, I don't got no *job*. I'm so *ashamed* of myself." Tears rolled down his cheeks; a spasm of despair rippled through his body.

Now it was my turn. Standing there in my well-scrubbed youthful innocence, my make-this-world-safe-for-democracy righteousness, I suddenly felt dirtier than he was.

Then the train arrived at my stop. As the doors opened, I heard the old man cluck sympathetically. "My, my," he said, "that is a difficult predicament, indeed. Sit down here and tell me about it."

I turned my head for one last look. The laborer was sprawled on the seat, his head in the old man's lap. The old man was softly stroking the filthy, matted hair.

As the train pulled away, I sat down on a bench. What I had wanted to do with muscle had been accomplished with kind words. I had just seen Aikido tried in combat, and the essence of it was love. I would have to practice the art with an entirely different spirit. It would be a long time before I could speak about the resolution of conflict.

~

Conflict in social action comes in many forms: brute force, implacable institutions, internal divisions among one's comrades. If there's an opening in the situation, a way through toward resolution, we're going to have to be very quiet so as not to be at the reactive mercy of each passing thought. We have to listen very carefully: for the uniqueness of each individual, including ourselves and all the various levels of our being; for the way in which fear and polarization outside reflect what is within us all; for ways in which, as Kabir says, we can "do what [we] do with another human being, but never put them out of [our] heart."

It takes the split-second timing of the quiet mind, working in harmony with the open heart, to know just when and how to say "Hey!" to a potentially dangerous opponent. So we work to be clear enough to seize the time. If you're a union leader in a tough collective bargaining session, for example, you'll want to catch that moment when it's best to yield a little, or when to shake your head "No deal." If you're working in a peace movement, timing will be crucial: when to call a national action, when to concentrate on local efforts; when to work on legislative opinion; when to confront the central government. With so much at stake, we need to strengthen that spacious awareness which allows us to take in *all* the elements of a political situation.

This applies particularly to one's opponents. We can't afford to get lost in reactivity and polarization. Quite the contrary, in fact. To hear the best possible labor settlement, you somehow have to be "in" the corporate negotiator opposite you at the bargaining table: what's it like to have to worry about chief executive officers, stockholders, the hierarchy and narrow options of corporate life? To hear the best possible strategy to bring about disarmament, you have to understand the mentality of those who plan for war: what fears, what models of mind, engender and support planning for nuclear destruction? Ultimately, you must somehow know your opponents as you know yourself in order to deal with them most effectively as opponents.

These insights don't come easily. It takes a great deal to detach ourselves from our vested interests and opinions long enough to take in and really feel the views of those arrayed against us. It's hard to find a place where we can meet other than as opponents. As fellow sake drinkers, parents, football fans? Hawks and doves—we're both birds? Perhaps, but it's not always that easy in the midst of a struggle. Finally, it's the work of that natural human compassion which comes into play only when the mind isn't so busy reacting and justifying itself. We can't fake it, we've got to feel it. And that's possible only when we're quiet behind it all—engaged and active where necessary, but rooted in a greater appreciation of concord behind all the immediate evidence of confrontation. We reach for that state because we've an obligation not to miss whatever possibilities there may be for reconciliation. We also do it to make sure that if the battle must be waged, we'll be most likely to win, and with the fewest possible casualties.

~

The secret of Aikido is to harmonize ourselves with the movement of the universe and bring ourselves into accord with the universe itself. He who has gained the secret of Aikido has the universe in himself and can say, "I am the universe."

When an enemy tries to fight with me, the universe itself, he has to break the harmony of the universe. Hence, at the moment he has the mind to fight with me, he is already defeated.

Winning means winning over the mind of discord in yourself.... Then how can you straighten your warped mind, purify your heart, and be harmonized with the activities of all things in nature? You should first make God's heart yours. It is a Great Love Omnipresent in all quarters and in all times of the universe. "There is no discord in love. There is no enemy of Love."

UYESHIBA MORIHEI

~

There's a way to oppose and still be beyond opposition. There's a way to express viewpoints but remain outside the destructive clash of opinion. There's a way to call for justice but not get lost in constantly judging. And there is harmony beneath discord. From such a perspective we're more able to recognize what's appropriate. When an action is appropriate, when it's in the Way of Things, it has great power, the power inherent in the Way. This is the practice of what Don Juan refers to as "the Impeccable Warrior"—the one to whom appropriate action and skillful means simply become apparent after quieting and harmonizing his or her thought. In this work, we must not only include ourselves and our opponents. We need "to harmonize with the movement of the universe." As we weigh concrete choices, we must step back to see the total landscape with a perspective spacious enough so that every possible factor is accounted for.

Once, for example, when Gandhi's supporters were stymied as to what action to take next, Gandhi went off to listen. He listened for three months, much to the impatience of his supporters, and then he set off on the Salt March. He'd heard what this could mean to the Indian "salt of the earth." He'd heard how close salt was to their daily lives, how it came from the sea itself, nature's provision, and yet was taxed by the British. He'd heard that the masses would be moved by so simple a gesture as claiming the salt of God's sea. He'd heard that the British were vulnerable, public opinion at home was turning, labor unions were already sympathetic to the struggle. He'd heard that if he set out, alone or with a few followers, people would join, and joyfully. He'd hear that all he had to do was to start walking. . . . And people started following, more and more. And when they arrived at the sea, Gandhi bathed and purified himself, then took a handful of salt from the beach and just held it up. Within one month, seventy thousand Indians had been jailed for mining their own salt, with more ready to follow their example and no room in the jails. Gandhi had heard that there would be nothing for the British to do except back down, and they did. Just the right action, at just the right time, coming from the mind "harmonized with the activities of all things in nature."

But "The British must leave as friends," said Gandhi. There must be freedom for oppressor and oppressed alike, taught King. "Sit down here and tell me about it," said the old Japanese man to the violent drunk. *What kind of victory is it when someone is left defeated?* Another turn in an endless cycle of victors and vanquished; power to this one, then to the other; different players, same game? Do we just want to be right, or do we all want to be free?

We seek to initiate political action openly and consciously from the outset. As we encounter opposition and conflict, we try to find ways to disarm it or pass through it as skillfully as possible. But what are we looking for as the final effect of our efforts? What place for reconciliation?

Obviously, at one level, there's no guarantee that there can be a battle without winners and losers. There's no assurance, especially in social action, that what divides us won't seem most real; it's almost always how the game gets defined. So we fight hard for our views; there are important victories to be won, against opponents.

On the other hand, if we've not been driven by anger most of the way, we also may feel a little uncomfortable at seeing someone else either diminished or still polarized when some kind of outcome has been reached.

~

We had fought for several years, and on the night the Equal Rights Amendment passed in our state, I saw one of the women who had opposed us at the election headquarters. We were both monitoring the count. When the result became clear, she looked at me. I wanted to reach out to her. She was just another woman—equal rights for her too. She gave me this very determined look, without anger, but you knew she wasn't all that happy.

So I tried, "Well, back to the kids for a while?" She said, "Oh yes, homework has completely deteriorated in our house." And I said, "Mine too. Equal rights for dummies." She sort of laughed. And it was nice there for a moment. Then she said, "You know, it isn't over yet. We're going to win. You're not going to be able to get enough states to ratify." And that's where it got left. That thing about homework . . . it just evaporated. She walked off; I walked off. And that took a little off the victory celebration for me.

~

What's likely to be left in the wake of a political struggle is rarely clear. All too often it falls short of any fundamental kind of reconciliation. The carpetbaggers come down from the North to exploit defeated Dixie. The "war to end all wars" turns out to sow the seeds of the next one. Struggle and conflict, then, are no longer necessary evils entered into as a last resort. We've come to live that way. Polarization has become a kind of habit, always looking for new circumstances to feed on, almost an end in itself. When moments of potential resolution arise, we are, tragically, not strong enough to seize the opportunities.

Reconciliation is not some final *tactic,* a way to tie up loose strings. Reconciliation is not a peace treaty signed on a battleship. Reconciliation is a continuous state of consciousness. What Lincoln had in mind *throughout* was to save the Union. What Gandhi had in mind *throughout* was to free both colonized and colonials. What King had in mind *throughout* was to liberate everyone from the scourge of racism.

The only way it seems possible to achieve such goals—extraordinarily difficult as they are—is to remember, again and again, who we all are *behind* our terrible conflicts. Somehow we must be able to encompass the paradox that we are, in these battles, both enemy and friend alike. We may be humans with deep differences, but we are all humans, all God's children. In that, we are One. Perhaps we must fight . . . but we must never forget.

We can take hope that this essential truth is so deep that it can somehow be revealed even in the midst of conflict. The fire can sometimes be so intense that it burns its way through to a place where we suddenly remember, "My God, how did we get lost in this? This is all wrong. This is hell." A searing realization can set us free.

~

It was a simple raid on a village: "Suspected VC." Most of the time you don't see who you're shooting at. At best, maybe some scurrying little figure. You see the fire, but you don't see the people.

But this one time, I saw the guy. I mean, I saw him. He was that guy, that person. I didn't shoot. I didn't even think not to shoot. I just didn't shoot.

The guy next to me shot. And he dropped him. Then I

looked at the guy next to me and I saw him. *He didn't know whether to be proud at what he'd done or not. I just nodded; he could take that any way he wanted.*

Then I realized that . . . how can I say this? . . . that I saw everybody. I mean, the VC, and this guy next to me, and myself. And at that point there was no way I was going to be able to go out and fight anymore. I was going to be dangerous to my outfit, in fact; I wasn't about to be shooting.

So I went to the chaplain, and he talked to a shrink, and I did, and it went through some kind of channel, and I got sent to the rear somehow. Don't know how it all got through. But it did. And that was the end of shooting.

~

But we can't always wait for such moments. The recognition of our unity which prevents us from getting lost in our divisions is something we have to have a strong grasp on *from the outset*. Any of us who choose to enter the arena of social action must go deep to the place where we are One. And that vision must be profound and all-inclusive, an affirmation of heart and soul. It must be strong enough to stay alive, often under the worst of conditions.

PLEASE CALL ME BY MY TRUE NAMES

Do not say that I'll depart tomorrow because even today I still arrive.

Look deeply; I arrive in every second to be a bud on a spring branch,

The Way of Social Action

to be a tiny bird, with wings still fragile,
  learning to sing in my new nest,
to be a caterpillar in the heart of a flower,
to be a jewel hiding itself in a stone.

I still arrive, in order to laugh and to cry,
  in order to fear and to hope,
the rhythm of my heart is the birth and death
  of all that are alive.

I am the mayfly metamorphosing on the
  surface of the river,
and I am the bird which, when spring comes,
  arrives in time to eat the mayfly.

I am a frog swimming happily in the clear water of a pond,
and I am the grass-snake who, approaching
  in silence, feeds itself on the frog.

I am the child in Uganda, all skin and bones,
  my legs as thin as bamboo sticks,
and I am the arms merchant, selling deadly weapons to
  Uganda.

I am the twelve-year-old girl, refugee on a
  small boat,
who throws herself into the ocean after being raped by a sea
  pirate,
and I am the pirate, my heart not yet capable
  of seeing and loving.

I am a member of the Politburo, with plenty
  of power in my hands,

and I am the man who has to pay his "debt
  of blood" to my people,
dying slowly in a forced labor camp.

My joy is like spring so warm it makes
  flowers bloom in all walks of life.
My pain is like a river of tears, so full it fills
  all four oceans.

Please call me by my true names, so I can hear
  all my cries and laughs at once,
  so I can see that my joy and pain are one.

Please call me by my true names, so I can wake
up and so the door of my heart can be left
open, the door of compassion.

THICH NHAT HANH

When this vision is strong and durable—when it moves us, when we truly love it—then we can take it with us wherever we go. It becomes our practice. We remember the bottom line: *We're here to awaken from the illusion of separateness.* As we meet, as we plan, as we speak out, as we march . . . a consciousness of unity is quietly there, at the heart of our action. We call on it, in fact we look for it, in whatever comes up. And we do so not because it's useful, or generous, or conciliatory, but because it's true. Unity has to be what's most real in consciousness if it's going to have full power in action. Ultimately, it's got to be what we "are."

Then we do what we do, and what happens happens, and there's no ultimate certainty as to how it will all end up. We're engaged and active; but we're watching the process unfold as well. And it can indeed unfold lawfully.

~

The soul force is indestructible and it goes on gaining power until it transforms everyone it touches.

MOHANDAS K. GANDHI

~

I do not want to give the impression that nonviolence will work miracles overnight. People are not easily moved from their mental ruts or purged of their prejudice and irrational feelings. When the underprivileged demand freedom, the privileged first react with bitterness and resistance. Even when the demands are couched in nonviolent terms, the initial response is the same. So the nonviolent approach does not immediately change the heart of the oppressor. It first does something to the hearts and souls of those committed to it. It gives them a new self-respect; it calls up resources of strength and courage that they did not know they had. Finally, it reaches the opponent and so stirs his conscience that reconciliation becomes a reality.

MARTIN LUTHER KING, JR.

~

In other words, "We Shall Overcome" means all of us.

~

And so time came for the big antinuclear demonstration in New York City, June 1982—the largest in American history. There was your usual politicking in preparing for it: who the speakers should be, the text of the call, the banner at the front of the march itself, relations with the media—all of that. But it became very clear, very early on, the whole thing had a life of its own. People were realizing intuitively and independently that this was just the right thing to happen now, and they just joined up. You'd get these reports: five thousand from Cleveland, seven hundred from Tulsa, like that, but from all over the country. A woman in the Midwest called and said, "I've gone ahead and rented this bus, but I'm not sure anyone in town even knows about this march yet. Could you send me a few posters?" It was great. She just knew the bus would fill up.

The day before the march itself, we held a religious convocation at the Cathedral of St. John the Divine. It was the largest gathering of the greatest variety of spiritual traditions ever held, so they said. It was wonderful. And very funny too ... watching everyone trying to get into the cathedral and seated before all of us, presumably, were to ascend. You had Japanese Buddhists bumping up against Hopi elders bumping up against classy Anglicans. The devotional people looked all mooshy and heartfelt. The meditation squads were all cool and mindful. There was a tough Islamic contingent, and long Jewish Orthodox beards, and long Russian Orthodox beards. And assorted motley good souls of no particular affiliation at all. Ecumenicism Unleashed—God help us! You had to laugh. And it was the most beautiful ceremony I ever attended.

Total harmony of spirit. One pure statement after the next, and from the most senior and established and respected leaders of the planet's religions and faiths. One after another, now from this corner of the cathedral, now *from another; you weren't sure what you'd hear next, or from where.*

The next day, when we gathered for the march itself, there were so many people crowded into the side streets, waiting to join the main route, that it took four hours for the march to get going. What was most extraordinary, however, was the way in which people stayed in place right where they were. For four hours. "Here we stand." You had only the ground you were standing on—it was that close. You'd think there would be great impatience, restlessness, irritability, but none of that. It was patient joy.

People seemed to understand that the way we were standing our ground—in place, in peace—was as much a statement as the march itself. Maybe more. It wasn't just something we were doing. It was the way we were being. The power and potential of that was tangible. Everyone felt it. It was really happening. Having felt it, it was not anything you were likely to forget—for whatever actions are going to be called for on the longer march ahead.

~

7

Burnout

Mutual support feels most right when it's like passing around helpings of food at the table. It's all very spontaneous. One gesture follows another. There's little self-consciousness about asking and offering. And everyone gets fed. Yet most of the time we're not all sitting around together passing out helpings. Circumstance prevents us from making it to the same table at the same time. We can't always wait for that feeling of sweetness and spontaneity from which generosity flows so easily. When help is needed, it's needed. Someone's in trouble right now. Whether or not our heart is open or our mind is at rest, something has to be done.

Much of the time we're able to adjust to these conditions. But at certain points—whether as the result of circumstance or the unexpected consequence of choice—*helping out gets heavy*. The care of others starts to be real work. A growing burden of personal responsibility leads to exhaustion and frustration. We feel as if we're putting out more than we're getting back. And are we making any difference anyway? We're tired of being with needy people, and embarrassed or guilty about feeling that way. As our heart begins to close down, joy and inspiration give way to apathy and resignation. There arises a range of emotions and responses we've come to call burnout.

~

~ *I never dreamed it would be so hard.*
~ *Forget it—you just can't change anybody.*
~ *Why does it always have to be me?*
~ *You can't beat the system.*
~ *They might at least say thank you.*
~ *It's like holding back the tide.*
~ *I don't know how to say no.*
~ *We're not helping anybody; it's just another business.*
~ *I'm just going through the motions.*
~ *I don't even know what help is anymore.*
~ *Hey, what about me?*

~

A nurse pulls out an IV a little too abruptly; she's sick of sick people. A probation officer turns bitter and cynical; ex-inmates never learn. A volunteer stops showing up; he's been given too little responsibility. His administrator never goes home; she's got to do everything herself. A legal aid lawyer screams at the judge; her client is denied bail. We give up on our parents, our kids, our friends; there's no way, they never listen. We give up on ourselves; we just haven't the resources, we've nothing left for others, we're barely holding on ourselves.

The experience of burnout has a particular kind of

poignance. Having started out to help others, we're somehow getting wounded ourselves. What we had in mind was expressing compassion. Instead, what we seem to be adding to the universe is more suffering—our own—while we're supposedly helping.

As our society has become increasingly reliant on the work of helping professionals, more and more attention has been given to the constellation of experiences we refer to as burnout. Simply to acknowledge the problem has meant a great deal to those among us who might otherwise blame ourselves for accumulations of doubt, fatigue, or resignation. It's comforting to know these challenges come with the ground. Any number of practical strategies have grown out of shared experience and a body of research. We've become more skillful in anticipating and treating burnout early on, in reducing stress, in managing time with greater sensitivity. We take leaves of absence from the front lines of suffering. In mutual support groups, we share responses that left unexpressed would become increasingly corrosive and painful. We are learning more about helping each other to help.

Nothing may be more important, in all this, than being gentle with ourselves. Whether we're professionals working a sixty-hour week or simply family members called upon to care daily for a sick relative, facing suffering continuously is no small task. We learn the value of recognizing our limits, forgiving ourselves our bouts of impatience or guilt, acknowledging our own needs. We see that to have compassion for others we must have compassion for ourselves.

For those who must deal with burnout, then, increasing support and methods for change and renewal have become available in a growing body of specific and comprehensive literature and through direct counseling itself. With respect for this ongoing work, we would add a few thoughts that arise from our particular perspective on service.

Throughout this inquiry we have steadily been examining the value of stepping outside and reperceiving some of the problems we face. Reperception itself, we've found, has the power to transform situations. Things change as they are seen differently, not necessarily because we are busy altering circumstance. From these shifts in perspective, in turn, we ourselves change. As we reach a deeper sense of who we are, we discover how much more we have to give.

In this process, we've come to see the value of the Witness—that stance behind experience in which we merely acknowledge *what is,* without judgment of ourselves or of others. It is simply a fair witness to our humanity. For it to have sufficient power to penetrate the deeper and perhaps darker recesses of the mind, however, it has to be infused with a steady, conscious commitment to truth. This may reveal insights that are either unsettling or reassuring. But these are simply our reactions, there to be noted and let go of.

The ability to remain quiet and open—simply to observe, never to judge—is what prevents the Witness from becoming reactive and self-conscious. As we become more grounded in this practice, turning it to one or another area of helping activity, we discover shifts of perspective that not only lighten the load of service but change its character as well.

Under the persistent scrutiny of the dispassionate Witness, we may observe that seeds of burnout are often sown in how we enter into the helping act and in what we bring with us—our motives, our needs, our expectations, the models we have for ourselves.

On the one hand, for example, we can recognize the natural impulse of the heart as it reaches out to those who suffer, seeking to ease their pain without concern for cost. This is the recognition of kindred spirit, born of inherent compassion. How good it makes us feel, how true to ourselves.

But we also observe that there is more going on in the helping act than the spontaneous generosity of the heart. In the presence of the suffering of others and their insistent needs, we observe the mind's fear and defensiveness. We also see how uncomfortable we may be about many of the desires situations call forth—our needs to appear responsible, useful, powerful, moral, worthy, needed, and so on. We might prefer to deny these or hide them in the shadow of the unconscious, but our experiment in truth calls upon us to witness *what is*. So we must acknowledge the reality of a house divided against itself—the inner conflict between head and heart awakened by the helping act itself. This struggle produces toxins of fatigue and emotional confusion. Seeing this, we may be tempted either to suppress it or even to freeze. The goal, however, is to stay with the Witness, to let our reactions pass by and simply continue.

So perhaps we might go on to witness ways in which

our ego's agenda colors our working relations with others, perhaps even preselecting those we choose or are willing to work with. If we need to be seen as wise, we might be drawn to someone who likes to ask us questions. We might avoid someone else, needier but prouder, who might challenge us or force us to face our confusion. "Sure I'd like to help. I'd like to help *that one,* help *her*— the one who needs my guidance." Called upon to spend time with people who *don't* gratify our needs, we watch ourselves tune out, lose patience, and get bored.

Or we may notice how often, in the guise of service, we try to impose our values on another. Perhaps we give them a little sermonette—"Don't you see, you're really God's child, my dear?"—when what they really need, if we'd bother to listen, is just a little empathy—"Yeah, I feel lousy too. Let's take a walk and feel lousy together." When they resist our wise words and don't buy what we're selling, we turn them off: "Well, Lord knows I tried. If they'd only just listen . . ."

Looking more closely still, we might notice how we tend to manipulate people towards the fulfillment of our own motives and needs—and perhaps go on to justify this in the name of good intentions or "what's right for others." We feel we know better. Simply observed, stripped of its justifications, all this often looks as if we just want things our own way. The Witness notes how others sense this, feel coerced, and back off. In turn we ourselves get defensive, pull away, or rush forward in an effort to make amends. More embarrassment . . . and a cycle of reactivity that is bound, sooner or later, to wear everybody out.

Sometimes we may also note that the motives that the

experience of service awakens operate at cross purposes. We want to be patient with clients in a welfare system, but we'd like to be more than a simple caseworker; and since promotion requires evidence of productivity, we hurry our clients along. Or maybe we want to assist our kids with their homework, but we'd like to help them become independent too: what to do, which to choose (and we're tired to begin with)? Pulled in two directions at the same time, if we identify with either one, another part of ourselves has become our enemy—still more potential for frustration and despair revealed as we witness the play of intentions and desires.

Meanwhile, we take it all very seriously, because we are often so focused on how we're doing that we lose a certain lightness and freedom in our work. We see how often we live in anticipation, wishing away the hours, testing the winds, taking soundings, waiting for the payoff. The Witness, which functions steadily in the present, moment to moment, observes how focused we are in the future while only appearing to be active in the here and now. We see, then, how we deny the replenishment that comes from the sheer joy and spontaneity of service itself.

As it steps further back, meanwhile, the Witness observes how this play of motives and needs produces *doubt*, yet another component of burnout. We doubt ourselves because the messages of our heart and our mind seem so at odds . . . or because we're not really at peace with our reasons for our actions in the first place . . . or because we seem to need so much in return from what we thought was supposed to be a "selfless" activity. We hear ourselves thinking, "Maybe this isn't the right place after all" . . . "Maybe I don't have anything left to offer" . . . "Maybe I need to be helping myself." A thousand maybes, which taint each act and undermine that *wholehearted* participation in service which itself would dissolve the doubt.

Without minimizing the external demands of helping others, then, it seems fair to say that some of the factors that wear us down we seem to have brought in with us at the outset. Along with our clean shirt, good intentions, and eagerness to serve, we've carried to work a number of needs and expectations. Sometimes burnout is simply our motives coming home to roost.

Inevitably, as these observations take hold, we may be tempted to question ourselves and react. But if we can stay grounded in the essential unjudging character of the Witness . . . if we can just hold on and listen . . . we can draw some useful conclusions and move further towards a greater sense of perspective.

~

God bless my mother, and God bless me. We made it through.

She had a stroke and a long period of rehabilitation, and it was clear she was going to have to stay with us for a while. I had all these things in mind: it was a chance to pay her back for all those years. There were these things I was going to help her clear up, like the way she was thinking. I wanted to do the whole job very well, this big opportunity. We should all feel good about it at the end. Little things like that. Some "little"!

Fights? Classics, like only a mother and daughter can have. And my mother is a great fighter, from the Old

How Can I Help?

School of somehow loving it and being very good at it and getting a kind of ecstatic look in your eye when you're really into it. I guess I'm exaggerating. It drives me a little crazy. I hate to argue. Oh, well . . .

But it got bad. Over a hard-boiled egg we had a bad fight. We'd both gotten worn out, irritable, and frustrated. Boom! I don't remember what about—just about how it was all going, and why her stay had gotten difficult and all of us had become more and more irritable and short-tempered.

In the middle of it, she stopped short and said, "Why are you doing all this for me anyway?" It sort of hit me, and I started to list all the reasons. They just came out: I was afraid for her; I wanted to get her well; I felt maybe I'd ignored her when I was younger; I needed to show her I was strong; I needed to get her ready for going home alone; old age; and on and on. I was amazed myself. I could have gone on giving reasons all night. Even she was impressed.

"Junk," she said when I was done.

"Junk?" I yelled. Like, boy, she'd made a real mistake with that remark. I could really get her.

"Yes, junk," she said again, but a little more quietly. And that little-more-quietly tone got me. And she went on: "You don't have to have all those reasons. We love each other. That's enough."

I felt like a child again. Having your parents show you something that's true, but you don't feel put down—you feel better, because it is true, and you know it, even though you are a child. I said, "You're right. You're really right. I'm sorry." She said, "Don't be sorry. Junk is fine. It's what you don't need anymore. I love you."

It was a wonderful moment, and the fight stopped, which

*my mother accepted a little reluctantly. No, I'm joking—
she was very pleased. She saw how it all was. Everything
after that was just, well, easier—less pressure, less trying,
less pushing, happening more by itself. And the visit ended
up fine. We just spent time together, and then she went
back to her house.*

~

By dispassionately acknowledging our personal needs,
we lessen their grip on our actions. More and more we
simply observe rather than identify with our motives. It's
not so much that we're trying to push them away; denial
buys us no peace. Rather, we're loosening our attachment to our motives by stepping behind them. It's not
that they aren't at play; we're simply offstage watching.
As this happens, our motives seem to lose some of the
mischievous, unpredictable power of their shadowy existence. From this vantage point we're more able to catch
sight of some need or expectation as it strives to move a
situation to its own gratification, setting us up for potential frustration. We can simply note it, not get lost in it,
and continue about our work with greater freedom.

By simply witnessing the character and conflict of our
reasons for helping out, then, we are making room for an
essential change of perspective. Our actions are less hostage to our needs. We can call upon a deeper, more universal source of action, one that is steady, reliable, less
likely to burn out. "We love each other. That's enough."

Meanwhile, the work of the Witness continues. Looking
further into what we bring to the helping act, we come

upon perhaps an even more fundamental cause of burn-out: *the feeling of personal responsibility; the sense that we are the authors of our actions; our identification of ourselves as the final source of the service.* We are the "doer" and we have to keep "doing" or nothing will get "done."

We identify ourselves as the doer in any number of ways. We may take difficulties or failures personally: "Oh God, these kids aren't learning to read at all. They'll never make it in society; I'm just not getting through." Or we may take credit for the accomplishments we seem to have been a part of: "Frankly, I just have to say it was a skillful diagnosis. You can trust these cases to me from now on." Or we may feel as if we've got to set people straight, we've got to get them to see: "My wife is so depressed. I really have to take her aside after the kids are asleep and show her what she's doing to herself."

We can see how often we define ourselves as "helpers," even to the point of buying into an illusion of indispensability. We become so invested in our work that we actually begin to equate who we are with what we do. It becomes a social mannerism, a way we introduce ourselves to one another. "Hello. What do you do?"

As we watch ourselves going off to work, then, it becomes a little like reading *The Little Engine That Could.* Up the mountain: "I think I can, I think I can, I think I can." Coming down: "I thought I could, I thought I could, I thought I could." Model train, maybe . . . but always climbing mountains . . . likely to run down sooner or later.

But all this can be witnessed. The same observation

that made it possible for us to note our reasons for acting can catch us in the process of identifying ourselves as the actor. We recognize how we're "taking things personally." We see how our self-esteem is riding on a particular job. It's clear how invested we are in a project, how each detail must bear our stamp, how we need to check and confirm every step, as if our very sense of identity were at stake. Of course, it can be.

But it needn't be. We've performed tasks in other ways than this before. We experience freedom from being the doer in those moments in which we are so *at one with our activity* (now with this child in the classroom, now with another; now at the bedside of one patient telling jokes, now in the next room hearing someone's grief) that it simply doesn't occur to us that we're "doing" at all. Everything's just happening. We're all action.

It's not always our efforts that burn us out; it's where the mind is standing in relation to them. The problem is not the work itself but the degree of our identification with it. It's doers who burn out. But we needn't always be doers. For as the process of witnessing becomes stronger—as we stay with it despite our reactions to what is being revealed—a subtle shift begins to take place in the direction of perspective and freedom.

If we persevere, our identification with the Witness grows while our attachment to being the doer seems to fall away. Quite remarkably, moreover, we also notice that while our identification as the doer is falling away, *much is still being accomplished.* We're still setting about our work, perhaps even more productively. It's just that we're not so personally identified with it any more. We see that in this state we're less likely to be frustrated, to feel rejected, to doubt ourselves, to burn out.

~

The sage does nothing, but nothing is left undone.
LAO TSU

~

As our perspective shifts we see, for example, a certain kind of lawfulness about our work. We see that needs reach for satisfaction, expectations seek confirmation, motives are just asking for it. Taking our initiatives personally means taking their consequences personally too. All these conditions seem inevitably to lead to frustration, fatigue, and burnout. That's simply how it all works.

In this recognition lies freedom. However much we remain conscious of this process, we're still in a state of awareness to catch causes of burnout as they seek to take hold. We can note them, and then let go. The process, moreover, is intriguing as well as effective. We can enjoy the Witness's revelations about the law and order of action even as we participate in the acting. It is as if we are functioning happily on two planes of consciousness at once. As a result, there can be peace where there was once agitation, confidence where there was doubt, trust where there was defensiveness and guilt, and abundant energy where there was burnout.

Freedom from attachment to our motives and from identification with the doer may seem high goals. Yet simply by holding them in consciousness, and *being com-*

passionate with ourselves in the process, we can turn burden-some situations into opportunities for growth.

While it is clear that what we bring into a helping situa-tion may lead to burnout, we ought not underestimate the external pressures. How often we find ourselves in environments or organizations that actually seem to make it harder to help others. What's natural and spon-taneous has now been rigidified by bureaucracy, rules, or standards of accountability. All of this can be incredibly frustrating, because it seems to constrict or thwart the very openness and sense of possibility that those who are suffering most yearn for—and those who wish to help out as well.

~

Here I am in this room with this woman who I know from when we painted the walls together and màde beds and worked in the kitchen, where she showed me a thing or two. And I know that those have been the moments when things have passed between us that are really good, really helpful, to both of us.

But right now, because I'm administering this house for the homeless, suddenly she's a "deinstitutionalized mental patient," and I'm having to determine how she's doing and whether she stays.

And it's like we're not alone in the room anymore. It's like there are these various ghosts around. There's the chairman of the advisory board in that corner ... the woman from the state agency in that chair ... the disgrun-

*tled folks on the floor are my volunteers . . . the fly on the
wall is a local reporter . . . and this nice guy whispering in
my ear is the minister of the local church, who's given us the
space. And they're all talking at once. About this woman.
"She's a potential success story." "Keep her here until we
can document it." "By any of the regulations she should
have been out weeks ago." "She's setting a good example
for new people." "She acts like she's a member of the staff."*

*Now I know from experience that this environment can
be mental chaos, probably crazier than the woman herself.
That's pretty terrible, given its power over her life. When
you're stuck in that, forget it. You're "institutionalized"
yourself.*

~

At the very least it makes sense to call upon the Witness
to "see how it all is"—to stop judging and reacting and
simply take in the total picture. So we see how the ad-
ministrators have to play it . . . or the volunteer's predicament . . . or the member of the board's game. As we
observe these roles, we're able to get a sense of what it
might be like to have to play any one of them. We appreciate how it all may have evolved, and the delusions that
led to it, and the confusions that perpetuate it, and the
accommodations that just plain had to be made. We see
why it is the way it is, and at as many levels as possible—
including the level at which it's utterly ridiculous and
hopeless and how-is-everyone-even-going-to-keep-it-all-
marginally-together-let-alone-help-or-be-helped. We're
living in the land of *Catch*-22.

The challenge is to turn it into *M*A*S*H*. Here we are
in the service, with a crazy war going on all around, no

idea when it will end, stuck every day with the same fellow idiots. Still we have to find some way to stay conscious. We'd better: Wounded people are coming in from out of the sky and they're screaming. So what do we do, Hawkeye? Just what a hawkeye is intended to do: hover above and survey the landscape. And then, as so many of us saw, episode after episode, when we're hard on the job, it's the one-pointed concentration of the surgeon . . . and the rest of the time we throw a party. We take in every absurd, contradictory, counterproductive aspect of the war zone and transform it into grist for irony, humor, irreverence, and creative mischief. That's how we stay nimble inside it. That's how we keep it from burning us out. Ultimately, that's how we turn it around.

Institutions are formalized mind-sets. These too can be witnessed. To become aware of those sets but see right through them from outside is the most reliable way not to get stuck or burned out by them. We master the rules, but we don't let them ultimately define us or narrow our field of perception. We encompass the craziness of the situation, so we can be skillful within it or playful when there's nothing to do but ride through the contradictions. Then we share a sense of the absurd with whoever else is inclined to see it that way. Whoever feels a little lost can find relief in our presence, in our tent, around our desk.

None of this means that we just suspend judgment forever. We observe . . . but there is action to be taken too. If we are serious in our criticisms of the practices and habits of helping organizations, however, we've got to be light, free, and sufficiently above it all to see where we can untangle the knots and bring about change. Everything is always changing anyway. With the perspective of the

Witness, we can see just which pressures, applied with the precision of a judo chop, can move the mass.

As frustrating and wearing as these situations can be, part of our service may entail taking some responsibility for them. The institutions we work in are going to reflect the sum total of consciousness invested in them at every moment. So it's "Our" problem. If it's "Us" who created it, it's probably going to have to be "Us" who'll shake it free.

Or maybe not. We can never be sure. We'll watch. Maybe it's not the right place to be putting our energies now. Maybe the inertia of the system is too great, its effect too strangling. Maybe we just need a break, some breathing space, a walk in the woods for some renewed inspiration. Maybe we're just tired. It's always right to be watching for that, always right to care for ourselves when we're seeking to care for others.

So perhaps we quit, not knowing where to go next, but trusting that the right vehicle to express our desire to serve will appear elsewhere, later. Are we going to place limits of circumstance on the expression of compassion?

Or perhaps we stay. If we do, we try to make sure that we're as conscious of everyone's situation as possible, and as alert to how the ground is moving from moment to moment, now obstructing this possibility, now revealing another one.

There may be no single remedy for the frustration and burnout that arise simply from the constricting situations in which we are often required to care for others. What serves us best is the expanded perspective that witnessing makes possible . . . and what it reveals from moment to moment. You do what you do when you can.

And when there's nothing to do, and burnout tries to rear its ugly head . . . you M*A*S*H it.

Burnout can arise, as we've seen, in what we bring with us into the helping act or what we encounter in the environment in which it's often conducted. Obviously, frustration and doubt occur too in the course of our work itself, particularly when we try to measure how it's all going.

Often, of course, assessment is called for. Sometimes the answer is clear: the wound is healing, the reading skills improving. Or we may want to look beneath these immediate consequences to deeper effects. You've established a development program in a small third-world village, but is it leading to self-sufficiency? You've comforted a friend, but did you reinforce his self-pity? You've exposed neglect in nursing homes, but did you do so in a way which will encourage them to reconsider how they think about society's elders? All this is a kind of appropriate continuing inquiry into practice, a sharpening of skillful means.

On the other hand, if our habits of self-observation are keen, if the Witness is active, we may note that our efforts to measure our work and ourselves are frequently patterns of insecurity.

"Did I help?" "Did it work?" "What did he feel?" "Why did she say that?" "What was really going on this morning?" "What if? . . . what if . . .?" "Try this . . . no, try that." "If only . . . if only . . ." And, probably heaviest of all: *"Was it really for the best? How do I know? How can I be sure? God, it's somebody's life!"*

All this is understandable. When suffering is at stake and we've offered ourselves to its relief, we naturally have an interest in how situations evolve. But sometimes this compulsive need to know leads us to doubt because we have a hard time coming to terms with the essential ambiguity of helping.

Paradoxical and elusive, service is ultimately a journey into the unknown. Did we really help? Help at what level? We often can't find answers. And we don't know what to do with that. So we wonder, worry, turn off, give up . . . or just struggle bravely on, puzzled and burdened, wearing down. See the helper? . . . He's the hard-working one over there . . . the one with the constant frown.

At some level this challenge is very plain. We can either be frustrated and worn out by uncertainty and doubt or try to find a way to open to the ambiguity, embrace it, work with it, be moved and inspired by it . . . and thereby come closer to the very heart of service where true freedom is found.

~

The hospital called our hot line service one day, and I was introduced to this man who seemed to be living outside of time, and we went through an experience which I still ponder.

A woman in her late eighties had just died. Her husband, who was reported to be a hundred and one, was stuck at home and was unable to bury her. So a few of us picked him up in a rented gypsy cab. He came downstairs very slowly, in a long black coat, a snappy hat, a cane, and gold teeth when he smiled—very mysterious looking. Antonio Lopez-Orlano. Quite a gentleman.

On the way to the funeral he told about Jacquelina. They'd met at a dance, lived together to help out during the Depression, fell in love later. How beautiful she was with her long black hair! When she died, she'd been in the hospital two months. She ran away to see him, but an ambulance caught up with her. They never said good-bye. When we got to the cemetery, he said, "I can't look. Open the casket, Raphael—take this photograph, tell me that it's her." It was.

When I took him home, I couldn't believe my eyes. He was living in an abandoned six-floor building, cold, dirty, garbage, smell of urine. "You *live* here?" "I do." "How many others?" "Just one; everyone left." "How long like this?" "Three years." I couldn't believe it. This man, around a century old, living in a freezing, abandoned building, during the coldest winters. I said, "Look, Antonio, I'd like to be your friend, come visit, see if I can help." He said, "Okay. If you'd like."

Four times a week for over a year I went, sometimes with my twelve-year-old daughter, Monica. And I'll tell you, it was so confusing, so many mixed signals. I wasn't sure whether I was coming or going, and to this day I wonder at how complex it was. What did it mean?

I worked to get him social security, food stamps, hot meals, and so on. He accepted them. And then he'd say, sometimes angry, sometimes just a little twinkle, "Stop meddling in my life." I'd bring people by to verify his eligibility for assistance. "They have to know who you are to help you," I told him. He hated that. "Who am I then? I know who I am." Then, when they'd come, he'd be so charming and witty, he had such finesse, and they'd leave amazed and in love with the hundred-and-one-year-old man who was living in this abandoned, freezing building. After they left, he'd look at me. "Before I met you I never had all these problems." He had me spinning. But I loved him. I truly loved him. He was a beautiful man.

He had this funny ritual if he thought I was coming on too strong. He'd tighten up his whole body and start heaving these heavy, gasping breaths, like he was being choked or having a fit. It was a great act. Monica and I took to doing it to each other at home. So I'd smile. And he'd say, "You're not taking me seriously." And I'd say, "I just can't figure you out." And he'd say, "I tell you, Raphael, you'll be the death of me yet." Maybe with a twinkle.

There were times when I wasn't sure whether to continue. How can you be sure if you're really helping someone or if you're meddling? I'd ask other people—social workers, friends. Who knew? I didn't. I don't think *he* really did. So I would ask for patience, great patience. "Lord, you sure are putting me through some incredible changes. I'm sure there's a reason behind all this, but I can't see it."

It became clear he'd have to move, and I found him a good place. But the day we moved was so painful. He was so angry, leaving his home. I felt so shitty. I arranged the furniture the same way, but it wasn't the same. Later, we had to give him a bath, which he agreed to but couldn't do alone. This was a very deep thing, to bathe him. We had to change the water five times. He felt humiliated, ashamed. I thought it was like a new beginning.

Then we noticed his toes, frostbitten terribly, three of them black. It scared him. "We have to go to the hospital, Tonio." Monica persuaded him. So the first night in his new home he was being set up to go to the hospital. He glared at me. "See."

They couldn't believe him there either. But they agreed to let him be treated at home and wait to see about amputation. Several weeks went by, and he started to complain of terrible stomach pains. He had to go back and be admitted. "Ralph, it probably wouldn't have happened if you hadn't moved me." Who knew?

They said he had advanced cancer. He went down and down. One night they called. "We think you should come." Monica and I went to him. I read to him from the Bible. Monica oiled his body. I said, "Antonio, you know we love you." He nodded, and then wanted to sleep. We left, and later he died.

We prepared a funeral, a very nice affair. Many people who had come to love this man attended. There I was at a burial again. I arranged it so that he was buried on top of Jacquelina. Then Monica and I went home.

What did it end up meaning? How much did I help, how much did I interfere? I don't know. How can you know what is the right true story of one man's time on earth? It's all a lesson. I did what seemed right in my heart. I tried to be patient. I loved this man.

Whatever else happened—the disruption of his life, the people and the programs, the new apartment, the bath, the hospital, my helping, his dying—I see it a little like that act of his: huffing and puffing and gasping, but playing. We met, who knows why, and we all did the best we could. Add it up, it was wonderful, just wonderful. It still touches me. It's still alive for me, still going on.

~

How unfamiliar the ground can be. How elusive the reasons that bring us together, at one moment strangers, at the next partners in the most intimate moments of life, following the impulses of the heart through unexpected turns toward unforeseeable ends. But where *does* it end? We meet, we help and are helped, then we go our separate ways. The helping act ripples out in time and space and beyond. How to follow its course and all its tributaries? How to measure it as it constantly moves? Who's to say where it stops ... and is one thing ... long enough to be named?

In helping others, we'll always find ambiguity and paradox. Sometimes these can just rip us apart and lead to self-doubt and self-consciousness, which if allowed to take hold will inevitably burn us out. How else might we deal with this need to know? Perhaps, once more, by remembering that the process of witnessing is focused essentially on *what is,* not what might be or could be. The Witness does not reach, grasp, or desire. Because it is an instrument of observation, not of need, it merely attends to things.

When we apply this to moments when our need to know is being frustrated, we experience yet another liberating change of perspective. We begin to allow, and embrace, the full beauty of the helping act *because of,* not in spite of, its ambiguity and paradox. Its mystery now only testifies to its ability to find its way into places we might never have imagined, to heal in ways we might not have intended.

In those moments when we are not at all sure what our actions have really amounted to, we can simply allow ourselves to be touched by what we *have* seen. So moving and poignant, the ways of compassion: an old man's dying body oiled by a young girl he'd only come to know in the last of his hundred and one years. Or perhaps there is no specific outcome to point to at all, only the feeling of having participated in something profound and wonderful. It does not lend itself to words or concepts, yet we know that it has happened. In mystery, we experience revelation.

With the perspective born of the Witness, then, we're able to hear when it's time to let things go and be what they are, as they recede beyond the horizon of our understanding.

At this point the need to know begins to fall away—and not simply because we've given up or resigned ourselves to ignorance. Quite the contrary: we've come into a deeper wisdom, which knows its place and accepts Not Knowing.

Here, after all, is where so much helping takes place anyway—in the land of Not Knowing. We do our work. We look to see what's happened, measuring it against past experience, the criteria of our training, the opinions of others, the still, small voice of intuition. We consult all these responsibly. Then we sit, and listen, and let it all fall into place. Sometimes it does, and sometimes it doesn't. Sometimes we hear how it all is; very often we don't. *Don't Know.* As frequently as this occurs, as much time as we spend Not Knowing, we might as well make ourselves at home there. We'll be that much less likely to burn ourselves out looking for what's beyond us. At best we may find pathways into a clearer practice of service.

For example, deep companionship, born of honesty, can often arise when we meet one another in Not Knowing. "What's the matter?" "I don't really know." "Well, I don't know either, but here I am." What's important, potentially even most healing, is that *we're being together in truth,* the truth of our present uncertainty. That mutual acknowledgment, and the sense of unity that comes of it, may make possible discoveries we'd never dreamed of in our efforts to figure it all out or pretend we understand. Humility turns out to be the threshold of insight.

If we can accept Not Knowing, we'll be less likely to get caught in models or theories, or attached to seeing things work out the way we'd like. More trusting of experience itself, we're more able to find new insights in new situations. The moments in which we come to the edge of the unfamiliar are less threatening. Our willingness to accept the unknown gives us courage. We can trip, fall, get lost . . . and still get up again and look around and start out once more. Confusion is now not an enemy; it's part of our regained innocence.

~

In the beginner's mind, there are many possibilities. In the expert's, there are few.

SUZUKI ROSHI

~

If we accept that the ends of our actions often prove unknowable, we're also freer to be focused on the process of our work as it's happening. We can be attentive to situations as they occur. What lies before us is it. Helping is right here. Not having to know so badly, not wandering off looking, we're more able to be present, freer simply to be.

We needn't be troubled or worn down, then, by paradox and ambiguity. The mystery of helping can be our ally, our teacher, an environment for wonder and discovery. If we enter into it openly, our actions fall into perspective, a larger pattern we can trust. At rest in the Witness, meanwhile, we greet the outcome of our action with equanimity.

~

A young woman in a small coastal village became pregnant. When questioned about the father, she didn't want to admit it was a young fisherman. Instead, she pointed to the monastery on the hill and named as the child's father a particular monk.

After the birth, the villagers took the baby up to the monastery and beat on the gate. When the monk came to the door, they said, "This is your child. It is your duty to raise it."

"Ah, so," said the monk. Then he took the child in his arms and closed the gate.

Nine years later, the same woman became ill and was approaching death. She did not wish to die with this lie on her conscience, so she admitted to the villagers that the young fisherman was the true father. Once again the villagers made their way up the mountain to the monastery and knocked on the gate. When the monk came to the gate, they said, "A great mistake has been made. You are not the father of that child. You need not raise the child any longer. It is our duty to raise it."

"Ah, so," said the monk . . . and gave back the child.

~

Here is a final shift in perspective which can help release us from burnout. We do what we can. Yet we cannot really presume to know the final meaning of our actions. We cannot help but see them against a larger backdrop in which the ultimate significance of a single life may not be clear.

So, at some level, we care with all our heart . . . and then we finally let go. We give it all we have . . . and trust the rest to God, to Nature, to the Universe. We do everything we can to relieve someone's suffering—our dearest's, our beloved's, anyone's—but we are willing to surrender attachment to how we want things to be, attachment even to the relief of their suffering. Our heart may break . . . and then we surrender that too.

This is the final act of service: to acknowledge and honor the integrity of another being as they, like us, pass through the beauty and the pain of a human birth. Its immediate meaning may surpass our understanding. But we are willing to keep the faith—which St. Paul describes as "the evidence of things unseen." Ultimately, all is well.

We play our part . . . and act . . . and burn out . . . and are helped or help ourselves to stand up again. As we struggle against the challenges and frustrations inherent in service, we will find good counsel, many methods, and much support. The particular approach we have shared is just one, to be called upon, as appropriate, in conjunction with others that ring true to particular needs.

The steps we have sought to emphasize, however, should become something more than corrective medicine, as useful as that is. They should embody health itself. We can do more than simply struggle to stay afloat;

we can discover a more reliable source of continuous buoyancy. We can do more than cope. We can see now that burnout need not always be an enemy. If not a best friend, it can at least be a catalyst, even a guide, for the inner work, the work on ourselves, which is the foundation of all true service, and the only way, finally, to maintain energy and inspiration. If we can view the places where we encounter fatigue and doubt as clues and signposts for that inner work, our journey will not only go more lightly but go further, deeper. We will not simply survive. We will grow.

Meanwhile, it will always serve to stay grounded in humble respect for all that is involved in the work to relieve suffering—a compassion for ourselves which is the source of compassion for all others. Whatever helpful hints for support and freedom we come upon must be tested against daily practice. We will slip and fall again and again. The struggle between heart and mind is fierce and continuous. The need to see suffering relieved is an essential ingredient of our humanity. Inevitably, we will feel the poignance and despair that arise on those occasions when affliction is not eased; indeed, it grows and spreads, cruel and ominous, despite all our efforts. The pain of the world will sear and break our hearts because we can no longer keep them closed. We've seen too much now. To some degree or other, we have surrendered into service and are willing to pay the price of compassion.

But with it comes the joy of a single, caring act. With it comes the honor of participating in a generous process in which one rises each day and does what one can. With it comes the simple, singular grace of being an instrument of Love, in whatever form, to whatever end.

How Can I Help?

~

We had just finished a six-week study tour of Kenya's major game parks, but our American college group had in many ways passed over what was most important to us: the people. So a friend and I set out on our own, feeling our way along the less-traveled roads for the pulse-points—the individual lives and feelings of the Kenyan people. Our trek took us to the small town of Kitale, and while resting our packs near the local market, a man simply walked up to us and introduced himself as Pastor Joseph.

Pastor Joseph, we discovered, was a Christian minister working in an area two hundred miles north of Kitale, where a drought had incarcerated the land and its people for three years. Pastor Joseph had collected some five hundred children who were entirely dependent upon him for their sustenance and shelter. We traveled with Joseph up into the drought area, to help him and to learn more about his work. Although we spent five days with him, a few moments tell the story.

We first approached Joseph's church around noon, after a two-day journey. Except for the children who scurried barefoot beside us on the scorching sand, the feeling surrounding us was of helpless isolation. It was a forgotten place—a vast, almost soundless plain. Thin, brown-skinned inhabitants moved like mirages on the baked white earth of this desert.

My friend and I were exhausted, but Pastor Joseph beamed as though a two-hundred-mile trek in a crowded, overheating lorry was routine. (It was, I found out later.) He stopped in front of a peeling, green cement-block structure. Squinting, we saw a small wooden cross peeking up above one edge of the warped tin roof. "This is my church!" exclaimed Joseph with irrepressible reverence. His sincerity made us feel ashamed not to see this homely clay form—a structure he found when first coming here—in quite the same way he did.

However, the "churchness" of that small, ingenuous structure became more apparent during our stay with Joseph, as did the enormity of his single-handed labor to look after the orphans of a starved, destitute tribe. We watched the sandy, famished faces of the children who stood outside the "church's" kitchen to receive their daily cups of maize. The same children stood inside it early Sunday morning, singing. Nothing I had ever seen looked less but felt more like a church. Two hundred Turkana tribespeople were packed, naked or half-clothed, on pews made of tattered scraps of wood set on desert stones. Pastor Joseph stood among them, leading the clapping and singing of strong, rhythmical hymns.

My friend and I, two strangers from across the sea, were welcomed into the church by all. As I reached down to touch the children's outstretched hands, I found that each child took a finger, then passed it along for a friend to hold. There was no fighting for my two hands, but, rather, a tacit understanding that ten fingers would, in time, be shared by all. We saw this same principle expressed by the children in many ways. For example, as the children were waiting for their cups of maize after the service, the cook brought out a crust of bread for one of the smallest, neediest children. He immediately looked for his friends, then began to break it in fragments to share with them. Seeing these children—experiencing them—I asked Joseph what he wanted most of all to do for them. A great smile lit up his face as he replied,

"To give and to give and to give, and to know that is my riches." He strode out in the desert, explaining his work to me. "I came here three years ago when the drought began." Pausing, he pulled from his pocket several folded notebook pages of children's names. "I have collected these children from all parts of Turkanaland. Their parents have died or are too weak to care for them. I walk out in the desert each day to search for children; ten, twenty, or thirty miles in a day. When I find a child who needs my help, I carry him over there." He motioned to a circular fence made of thorny acacia branches. "The children sleep within the fence when I bring them from the desert. I have wanted to build the children a shelter for a long while. But I find enough money only for food."

I listened to Joseph while drawing the last of my water from a half-gallon pouch. When I offered him a swallow, he smiled but refused. We had been walking under the desert sun for only an hour but already I was feeling weak. He glanced at my friend and me, sensing our condition, then led us to a shade tree as he continued describing his work. "When I go into the desert, I take nothing with me. I know that God is with me. I am going out to find *His* children, and I know that He comes with me."

With a simplicity, yet a spiritual toughness which has known and endured great suffering, Joseph told us of several long searches in the desert when he existed for days on edible desert plants and water sucked from their roots. Bowing his head, he added, "These are God's children I am seeking!"

The next day, we sat with Joseph in a corner of his church to do something we all knew was needed: pray. In the background, children sniffled, laughed, and cried—like punctuation marks between our prayers. We rarely spoke. When we lifted our heads and looked into one another's eyes, it was to affirm a strength growing in us all: the realization that indeed, our prayers were being heard, and that it was *natural* for them to be heard. We found ourselves in that incredible condition of trusting God, of sensing that there is a higher law to appeal to—and that it was available to all of us.

That afternoon it began to rain. For half an hour, rains poured down on the hard, white earth. The children huddled inside the door of the church and sat silent, watching it. I expected shouts of joy. But, instead, I heard an utter silence—the sound of reverence. Both Joseph and the children were perfectly quiet until the rain stopped. He bowed his head and told me, "This is the hardest rain they have seen in three years. They have seen their parents die because of the drought. What else can they do now but be still and watch?"

On our last night in Turkanaland we were served a supper by Joseph's friends, and told that he would return much later. We had spent the day with children at the church, and watched Joseph disappear at noon, carrying a coughing child across the desert.

One small candle flame flickered across Joseph's face as he walked into the church late that night, carrying the same child, now asleep in his arms. He gently laid the little one inside the door and came to sit beside us. Closing his eyes, he sat quietly for several moments until his breathing became easier. He looked utterly exhausted. He whispered, "There is no tomorrow here. There is only today and what God asks me to do today." We listened quietly as his voice grew. "Today I found a child who needed to be taken for special care to a place seven miles away. So I took the child there. But when I arrived, I found that two of the children I had carried there a few days before had died." His voice maintained its level. "So I will dig their graves tomorrow. And I am grateful to God that I can do that for these people."

Joseph's words hung in silence for a long while. They so overwhelmed me. I couldn't utter a word. I remember just bowing my head.

~

8

Reprise: Walking
Each Other Home

What is it that so touches us about a single caring act or a life surrendered into service? Perhaps we see our deepest yearnings reflected in others, and this encourages us to believe in our own purity and beauty. These are no longer just ideals to strive for. We can reach them, we can be that way. Images of compassion beckon and encourage us onward.

~

I went to Nicaragua as a Maryknoll missioner in 1971, before the big earthquake, and before the revolution. I had every expectation and notion about helping people you could imagine. It would bore you to tears to list them—and you'd probably understand every one.

I walked into this barrio, with three hundred people, an old cotton farm, incredibly hot and barren, three trees near an old hacienda, then miles of nothing but small bushes. The idea was to help build it up from there, make room for others. I'd be part of that effort, and part of those people.

It wasn't too long before I realized I was signing up for the course: Life 101. First assignment: the horror of poverty, which until then was something I'd only known about from the eyebrows up. No running water, no electricity, malnutrition, disease. People lived in big one-room houses made from materials we'd throw away in the States. We had to haul water from miles away. Dirty water was kept in a hole in the ground where it could be saved to keep the dust down or wash the patio. It took me a while to tell the difference between a clean dirt floor and a dirty dirt floor.

But people rarely complained. Not that they were saints and martyrs, but the grumbling was always in a here-we-are-let's-make-the-best-of-it manner. There was just this moment-to-moment quality to their life. First lesson for me: you do what's in front of you, you start where you are.

Second lesson: Who do you think you are, anyway? Because you go in and you're going to help someone, and then all of a sudden you see they're a lot stronger than you are in certain very important ways. And how they're acting has to do with who they are, especially down there. Who they are is all they have—no possessions, no property, very little to protect.

So I go into someone's hut for the first time, wondering how they could live under such conditions, and I'm embraced by this lovely woman who gives me her only chair and spends three hours talking, and when am I coming back? I cannot believe her liveliness and purity of heart, and she awakens me to my own. So I see that service is beauty.

Or a kid comes by and asks to dust our car. We see him

later, peering in the window as we're preparing our main meal. So we invite him in, as payment, and pile his plate high, and he's eating like there's no tomorrow. And then he suddenly hears some other kids outside, and he catches himself and takes the food out to them. And I'm blown away. I see that service is remembering.

Or I'd feel uncomfortable about the comfort of our own house; nothing special, but we have beds, not the boards they slept on, and some semblance of privacy, like they'd never known. But they'd come in—"Isn't this beautiful? Oh, it's so nice"—without the slightest envy, without anything but appreciation on our behalf. And I see that service is gratitude.

Or that service is truth and honesty. Because part of me is romanticizing all this a little. I have to accept that and listen to who I am and be myself all along the way. Because we're all taking the course, right? But we have different assignments. And so finding common ground helps. Gossip and small talk are important. To sit on a patio in the evening and talk about nothing and say everything. Service is chitchat.

And service is death, too. You die in service, and you die into service.

They told us the insurrection was to begin a day or two beforehand. Someone came by: "The revolution is going to start tomorrow. What are you going to do?" And in our case, we were ready. At that point, if you weren't for Somoza, you were supporting the Sandinistas. We'd opted for them because from what we'd seen over the years, the signs of the kingdom were more likely to be realized: fraternity, justice, help for the overwhelming majority of the poor.

And we'd prepared, and organized civil-defense support, and had the chance to learn how to handle a gun, although I didn't feel that was being asked of me.

That evening we had to notify the fathers and the sisters, and we buzzed off in our Jeep to see the Franciscans. At about six o'clock, we heard homemade bombs go off, and machine guns, and heavy fire. We hit the floor in this flimsy asbestos house. Here it was.

An hour later, someone from the Sandinistas rushed in: "Come quick, we have a wounded *compañero!*" It was Armando, shot in the arm—not someone we knew from church, but we knew he was a leader. He was lying there, bleeding in the road. I began to panic. I'd never seen blood before. But my friend, another sister, told me to squat down and hold his arm and she'd go get medicine.

All of a sudden—"There's a car coming!" National Guard or Sandinista? Everyone else dived behind this pathetic asbestos wall. Armando and I were there in the road, looking at each other. One of those moments: "Okay, here we are. What am I going to do?"

I'm thinking, "How'd I get here?" and "Where's Julianne?" and "Who the hell is in that car?" and "MOM!" And finally, "Well, if I'm with them and they're willing to die, I guess it's all right, and I'll be willing too. Just don't tell my mother." The car drove up. It was friendly. And as he was being bandaged up, Armando and I looked at each other for a quiet second—a kind of acknowledgment—and that was that. He started giving orders again. Then the madness took over.

People came through all night. They brought in kids who died. I'd never seen death before. Their friends would stand around, not knowing what to do. One boy died in my arms.

They brought him in all covered with blood. I knew his face but not his name. He was still breathing. But when I lifted him up on a table, he gasped three times and shuddered and gave up the ghost. On the last breath, he really let go. He was so young—soft hands. Nobody knew his name. It was a very sad moment, a still moment. And that was very good for me—very deep, but very, very sad.

Then the fighting started to get heavy again. Everyone went down on the floor. The kids were so frightened, saying prayers and crying. The body was on the floor. But nobody wanted it discovered on their property; it could get them in trouble with the Guard. So he was thrown into a hole, with just a shroud over him. And I thought, "He died of such violence—couldn't he even get buried?" And I felt all his innocence, and the meaning of his death, and the cost of freedom, and the horror of war. And I thought, "God is supposed to call everyone by his true name. So what's his name?" And you find yourself saying the Our Father and shaking your fist at the sky at the same moment. And then you're done with that. And you bandage wounds because there's nothing else to do. That's the dying into service.

So what was his name? Who was he? Who were they all? Well, they were people who were allowing me to be there with them. They were sharing life and death and hope with me. And they were sharing faith. And they were sharing that they didn't know what to do with it all any more than I did. And they were helping bring me an experience of God too, a God who works through people. Because I was seeing "No greater love hath a man than to lay down his life for a friend." I saw that. I saw that happen.

So you say you're going to be with people and you're

going to help. But what does that really mean? It turns out to be an endless series of questions. What do I really hold to be the truth of my life? What do I have to give, and what am I called on to give? How am I a part of human history and great moments of change? Who am I? And where is God in all this?

That's who he was, that boy; that's who they all were. They were those questions. Part of me has become those questions. We are questions for one another. And service is exploring them and awakening through them.

How do I measure what it means to have been given all that?

~

So service is "an endless series of questions," puzzling and insistent. It not only raises questions, it helps to answer them. Service is a curriculum.

In this curriculum, we encounter our own limitations—a number of which we have met in the course of this book. We have seen, for example, how our ego can lock us into narrow self-images, leaving us tentative and hesitant to reach out. Our resistance to pain can lead us to insulate ourselves from suffering. When our hearts do open in empathy, all too often we close down quickly, frightened by the intensity of our feelings; we substitute denial, pity, or other defense mechanisms for the spontaneous response of the heart. Frequently, we find ourselves so identified with our own needs that we tend to treat others as objects to be manipulated toward our own ends. We see how the restlessness of our minds can hinder our ability to listen; we find ourselves at least one thought away from someone else. And when we try to help through social action, we often so identify an opponent as an enemy that we remain locked in a cycle of recrimination. Meanwhile, as the toxicity of these and other hindrances builds up, we begin to wear down. We burn out. Helping starts to hurt.

But the curriculum of service provides us with information about our strengths as well, and we discover how these contribute to genuinely help-full service. Each time we drop our masks and meet heart-to-heart, reassuring one another simply by the quality of our presence, we experience a profound bond which we intuitively understand is nourishing everyone. Each time we quiet our mind, our listening becomes sharp and clear, deep and perceptive; we realize that we know more than we thought we knew, and can reach out and hear, as if from inside, the heart of someone's pain. Each time we are able to remain open to suffering, despite our fear and defensiveness, we sense a love in us which becomes increasingly unconditional.

As we close our inquiry into service, then, we can see in this mosaic of limitations and strength a still deeper teaching. Common to all those habits which hinder us is a sense of separateness; we are divided within ourselves and cut off from others. Common to all those moments and actions which truly seem to help, however, is the experience of unity; the mind and the heart work in harmony, and barriers between us dissolve.

Separateness and unity. How interesting that these root causes, revealed in the experience of helping, turn out to be what most spiritual traditions define as the fundamental issue of life itself. Awakening from our sense of separateness is what we are called to do in all things, not merely in service. Whether these traditions speak of us as being cut off from God, Nature, Original Mind, True Being, the Tao, the Dharma—they call on us, in one voice, to undertake the journey back to unity.

Service, from this perspective, is part of that journey. It is no longer an end in itself. It is a vehicle through which we reach a deeper understanding of life. Each step we take, each moment in which we grow toward a greater understanding of unity, steadily transforms us into instruments of that help which truly heals.

Service not only reveals a larger vision of life, but steadily moves us along and supports us in our efforts to realize this vision. Each time we seek to respond to appeals for help we are being shown where we must grow in our sense of unity and what inner resources we can call upon to do so. We are constantly given, for example, the chance to experience the inherent generosity of our heart. Each time this happens, our faith in that part of ourselves which is intimately related to the rest of the universe is strengthened. So, too, approaching each act of caring with a desire to grow, we also meet our fears and resistances—but with the opportunity to see them for what they are, and, in so doing, to loosen their hold and ultimately to relinquish them. *On the path of service, then, we are constantly given feedback which helps us along the greater journey of awakening.*

All the methods we have discussed throughout the book support us in this effort. They are, it turns out, more than helpful hints to improve the quality of service. They are appropriate technology for loosening the hold of separateness and for strengthening our vision of unity.

For example, we may start out to quiet the mind simply to hear the needs of others. To do so we learn to identify less with our own thoughts. Listening more, judging less, then, there is less divisiveness in our awareness. As we loosen our identification with personal motives and models of self, meanwhile, our awareness becomes more panoramic and inclusive; we're freer to take in more and more. Under these conditions, in turn, all our mental faculties can come into play as needed— memory, training, logic and analysis, intuition, wisdom. Unexpected connections become apparent. We may recognize deeper patterns in the events which are unfolding. As we continue, we may even begin to gain insight into a larger order of lawfulness we cannot understand rationally but which nevertheless resonates within. We come to sense the Way of Things (Tao) of which our actions are but a part. The hold of separateness is thus being broken at its source, in our own mind.

These practices open us up to an awareness within ourselves *which is itself unitive*. Not only do we see and hear more, but our very openness and spaciousness dissolve opposition and discord.

Through these practices, and our efforts to keep our hearts open in the presence of suffering, we find ourselves more available to whoever we are with. Compassion is increasingly an automatic response. We find a deep quality of love infusing our actions with others. The expression of this love, in turn, becomes increasingly our goal, whatever the circumstances. The more unconditionally we share it, the more helpful it is to all.

This is the essence of the spiritual path of devotional service. One enters into the helping act not only because there is a need to be met. Service gradually becomes an offering, first to those we are with, but eventually to that greater truth or source of being in which we are all joined in love. Helping becomes an act of reverence, worship, gratitude. It is grace merely to have the chance to serve.

Mother Teresa, for example, bending to hold a dying leper, sees there only "Christ in a distressing disguise." She's not "helping a dying leper," she's loving God, affirming in whomever she's with universal qualities of perfection and beauty. One can imagine how it might feel to be held in this spirit during one's final moments of life.

The Hindu deity Hanuman offers a similar example of devotional service. Every act he performs becomes an offering to Rama (God). His service brings him to the very edge of unitive love. How powerful his vision: "When I know who I am, I *am* you," he says, kneeling before Rama, "when I don't know who I am, I *serve* you."

For both of these inspirational figures, and for any of us, the smallest acts of caring—making a sick friend's bed, filling a bowl on a soup line, welcoming a stranger, comforting a frightened child—can be a means of affirming the greater unity of life in love. As real as this spirit is in us, we have to communicate it to others, in addition to everything else we are doing on their behalf.

Placing service in a spiritual perspective in no way diminishes what we have to offer others through training, experience, individuality, special skills, or sense of humor. Quite the reverse. Our particular talents and unique qualities are likely to come forth more reliably when we have a richer and more spacious sense of who we are—the very promise of all spiritual practice.

To the question, "How can I help?" we now see the possibility of a deeper answer than we might once have expected. We can, of course, help through all that we *do*. But at the deepest level we help through who we *are*. We help, that is, by appreciating the connection between service and our own progress on the journey of awakening into a fuller sense of unity.

We work on ourselves, then, in order to help others. And we help others as a vehicle for working on ourselves.

In this recognition, we find new freedom and opportunity. External obstacles and old habits—our past experience of service—can now be dealt with in the broader context of our own growth. And each step we take out of the illusion of separateness, we now can see, will inevitably be a blessing to ourselves and all we are with.

In our initial impulse to help out, had we really anticipated so rich a path?

As we take to this path, however, we find it neither straight nor smooth. At moments we may become profoundly aware of our oneness with all things. Our sense of possibility expands. Could it be like this more often . . . . more often than not?

But then some incident or situation arises and we are thrown back into the pain of separateness once again. At first this must shock us; we thought we were farther along. Yet, after a moment's pause at the side of the road, a break for a little self-pity and self-recrimination, we have nothing to do but take up the journey once again. Though the road is circuitous, the transformation proceeds inevitably. Gradually we come to sense profound changes in who we are. Our hearts can open and our awareness expand only so far and so often before we must conclude that we are somehow more than we once believed.

How much more? This is for each of us to discover, walking the path at our own pace. The general direction, however, seems clear. Gradually, as our practice continues, *the fact of our unity becomes more real and powerful to us than the belief in our separateness.*

We may discover this in the course of ordinary daily work. In a demanding situation we may quietly affirm the fact of unity and suddenly see a breakthrough or insight follow as a result. Or we may come to recognize how our relationship with others has altered; how much more aware we are now of what we have in common than what once seemed to have set us apart.

Or we may experience moments of enlightenment or revelation which defy description. These may be more difficult for us to understand. They may happen instantaneously, and then become less vivid, and fade away. But their impact is such that they are never forgotten, and everything thereafter looks different. In referring to these transcendent moments, some speak of having lost a sense of the individual self altogether, or of having come to see, with undeniable certainty, that who we are is Spirit, beyond form. From such a vantage point, however it is described, *separateness is seen to be a creation of mind.* All really *is* One. Such is the testimony, in any case, of what has been "seen."

It is out of these transformative experiences that we

find ourselves able to accept a number of seeming paradoxes. We are in the world but not of the world. We are a part of what is formless but we are in form. We exist beyond the polarities of positive and negative, dark and light, good and evil, pleasure and pain, yin and yang; but we function under their cloak as well. Even our perspective on separateness has changed. For while it may indeed be a "delusion of consciousness," even this delusion seems part of a greater order. It seems to be in the way of things that we develop our initial identification with a separate self and go on to get lost in it. It seems also to be in the way of things that we ultimately come to appreciate this predicament and go on to resolve it. We do so, however, not by returning to an innocence which existed before we felt ourselves to be separate. Rather we grow toward integration, a balance in which we can work within our separateness while resting in the greater unity which lies beyond it.

Separateness is there . . . to be awakened out of. Service is a perfect vehicle for this awakening.

We look at our present condition now with great compassion for ourselves and for the work we have taken on. We see the beauty of our humanity in the light of our divinity. From this vision comes a fullness of heart and a profound willingness and eagerness to come to one another's support.

~

O, that my priest's robe were wide enough
to gather up all the suffering people
In this floating world.

RYOKAN

How Can I Help?

~

Ultimately, on this journey, we simply become compassion, as a natural consequence of what we have seen and understood.

~

Once his brother asked Ryokan to visit his house and speak to his delinquent son. Ryokan came but did not say a word of admonition to the boy. He stayed overnight and prepared to leave the next morning. As the wayward nephew was lacing up Ryokan's sandals, he felt a drop of warm water. Glancing up, he saw Ryokan looking down at him, his eyes full of tears. Ryokan then returned home, and the nephew changed for the better.

> *One Rose, One Bowl*, JOHN STEVENS

~

What once seemed work now can be a kind of play...re-creation...a joyous participation in the unfoldment of life and form.

~

I watch these little kindergarten kids, all eager and into their little world, and sometimes they dissolve into little molecules, bounding around, vital and energetic, and the classroom becomes a kind of organism. And it's so wonderful and comical and so great that, for a moment, I see the whole human condition that way. It's all like a joyous creation in which the gods and goddesses are taking delight. So why shouldn't we? And I'll just plunge into the dance.

"Clara, you take the triangle, Margo you have the drum, Stevie has a whistle," and I pick up the tambourine.

Sometimes I'll carry this feeling home with me, and I have it around the house. I feel it at work inside. I'm cleaning up, and calling this friend and that, and dropping in on a person down the hall, and helping them out with whatever. And it's like the only reason to be here at all is to play. And the fact that this take on things makes me and everyone else feel so good will make me stop for a moment and think, "My God. Maybe it's true."

~

This is the vision spiritual traditions offer: service as a journey of awakening. The value of such a perspective on our work is not so much that it leads to exalted states and indescribable experiences. It is enough that it can help keep us straight.

Nothing is "spiritual" just by calling it so. "Unity" will finally mean something to us only as the felt truth of direct experience. But this seems to be where it is so often revealed: in what is most familiar to us as human beings, in what we can most readily understand and appreciate because we find it so touching, comforting, and uplifting. We find it in the power and beauty of a single, simple caring act.

~

Take a look around. We're the only building left on the block. All the rest is rubble from urban renewal. We got some renewal going on here, though. We call it Project Return. I helped set it up, but now it has a life of its own.

How Can I Help?

What's going on at this moment, as you can see, is what you might call Bilingual Bingo, what with the different languages and accents some of these elderly people speak. Look at it. Sometimes it'll take five minutes for a single number to get around the room. Different languages; some folks are a little deaf or distracted or confused; two ladies are into an argument; this one is always cheating; three people yelling "Bingo!" when we haven't even pulled enough numbers for it. It's insane; it's just great. And don't tell me this isn't how the whole world is running, by the way. I see this as an average situation. Excuse me—Richard, Mrs. Schwartz is looking for her coat.

So ... these boys moving around like waiters at a fancy restaurant, flirting up these old ladies, putting on their sweaters, reminding them of their numbers ... these guys were heavy. I mean *heavy*. Years of crime, dope, doing time. They're in a program called Prodigal. Last shot for rehabilitation. Miss this one, you're done; no more programs. And I bring them over here to this Senior Citizens Center to give them a chance to make that last step home by looking out for someone beside themselves. Because maybe this center's a last shot for some of the old folks too. Last shot for companionship, last shot before dying, alone. Both groups on the edge—why not bring them together?

Of course, people were a little skeptical at first. "Ex-junkies, ex-cons, helping old ladies? You gotta be crazy. They're out there mugging them, man," is what they said initially. Then I'd say, "I see that, but think about it a little more. How are we going to stop this madness? I see something in this idea for everybody. Chance to break out of the old patterns. We'll pull everybody just a little more out of

their thing." Well, it was different enough for them to give
it a chance . . . as simple as the idea really is.

So look around. There's so much life here I think it's
going to explode sometimes. And strange moments too.
Some guy comes up to me and says, "That lady over there,
she looks like someone I done one time." I say, "Go ask her
if there's anything she needs." And he does. And I'm
amazed. I can't believe it myself, and I set up this scene, this
crazy little world here. I mean, the idea came around anyway. The old people and the kids, they're actually doing it.
Talk to them, listen to them.

~

I come to this center for company, I suppose, older women
like myself. But I meet these boys here. Very interesting,
very different than I expected. This young man who walks
me home, he's a very nice boy. His mother, she should be
proud of how he acts with me. I know he's done wrong.
Look, they did it to me. One kid once put a gun to my head
and went for my diamond ring and wedding band. He bit
my finger to try to get it off. But you know what? I wasn't
angry. Maybe he never had any parents—who knows what
happened when he was very young, who knows?

I had some terrible experiences when I was young. Poverty and war. World War I. I was ten years old. The Ger-
mans dropped bombs. A woman jumped on me to protect
me. Her body was ripped in half. She saved my life. I was
very frightened after that. I'm frightened now. But I'm
grateful for life, although it's a little lonely.

But this boy . . . he walks me home. He helps with my
groceries. He says, "Wear lipstick, a nice dress. You're very

pretty. You should get married again, a nice lady like you. That man in the center, he wants to get married again." "He's not good enough for me," I say. "You're right," he says, "Marry me." "You're good enough," I say. "But an old Jewish lady and a young black criminal? What would they think?"

I don't know what he sees in me, to be so nice. All I know, he walks me home. We talk and joke. I learn things about how things are in the world now, which I don't know much anymore. And I don't get the feeling that I'm just a little old Jewish lady. You think that's nothing? You know how many other people I don't feel like a little old lady with? None. Nobody. That's the truth. How's that?

~

Try to shake having been a junkie and done time, man. Everywhere you go, you get that. That's who you are. But this woman, it's like she doesn't care. She says she had a hard life too, maybe that's it. I told her how I robbed things. I told her about jail. She says, "Your mother must have been very upset. Let's get groceries. You have time to do that?" Nobody ever treated me like I had anything to give. Just to take. So that's all I ever did. Take.

Never knew my folks, started in when I was nine, four juvenile institutions, two escapes, on the street at twelve, dealt heroin, burglary; by fourteen I had my own car and apartment. Got caught. Did a three-year bid in prison. Had to stay in the hole because people try to sodomize me. One guy stopped some other heavy guy trying to sodomize me and got cut bad doing it, cut real bad. Only time anybody risked anything for me.

This woman, she shows me something. I seen jive cour-

age, but she's brave, living all alone, being old. She doesn't recognize just how much she understands about life. Ain't nobody ask her questions anymore now, so she forgets how much she knows. I ask her questions. I'm curious. She's interesting. We learn things together just looking around on the street. We have a good time. And I done a lot of time.

Old or young, no difference. I'm twenty-five and I feel old. My voice sound old on the phone, they say. So old people, I understand their situation a little. They're scared, I been scared. They live alone, like in a cell. I lived alone, in a cell. So this place, this attitude toward life they got going in this center, it's showing me some things. And this woman too. I'm not who I always thought I was being with her, just walking her home. Her too, probably. It's like you're free for that period. I said, "You're going to have me born again." She said, "That's not for Jews." I've done enough time. I've done enough taking. Time to be free.

~

Here we are, in the end, fellow beings on the journey. We come together or are brought together in so many ways. Some seem extraordinary: a clown peers into the crib of a child burned beyond recognition: a literacy tutor and a prisoner in solitary keep a conversation going through a food hatch in the midst of a small riot: a North American nun and a Nicaraguan revolutionary lie together in the road, awaiting possible death.

Others seem as simple as these are dramatic and still are as powerful: a social worker and a bag lady sit together in the park in the rain; an old Japanese man comforts a drunk on a train; a therapist and a patient hear a bird.

And sometimes the circumstances are so ordinary we think nothing of them at all, or only in rare flashes appreciate the beauty of their everydayness: putting a child to sleep; talking to a neighbor waiting for the light to turn green; exchanging glances with a fellow overworked employee.

Here we are then in these forms, helping within our appointed roles, easing the pain of body, heart, and mind, working for peace and justice. And yet in the course of all this, we really *do* go beyond identification with all that would define us as "other." We really *do* meet behind our separateness. And for however long that lasts, such meeting is what helps . . . helps at the level of being . . . *is* help itself. We are sharing the experience of unity. We are walking each other home.

There is no reason why we cannot bring this quality to any human exchange. Any act that can be performed in the spirit of unity can turn out to be helpful.

There's no place special we have to be in order to help out. Right where we are, in whatever we're already doing, the opportunity to be of service is almost always present. We need only stay conscious and aware, and then give whatever we can to whoever is right there.

It only remains to add that we can be helping immeasurably when we are all alone. Each moment in which one of us grows in the awareness of our unity and divinity blesses us all. "We" are becoming that much more aware. While the action that comes from that awareness is critical, this moment of growth in true compassion is helpful *in itself.*

Meanwhile, it's useful to hear how much helping is taking place and just how much it can mean.

~

I tell you I would have died but for the friendships.

The doctors had just about given up. Forget it for having any will to live. I can't begin to describe the despair. Beyond the relentless physical pain, there was this utter emptiness of heart and soul. Each morning felt like waking up in hell—can you understand that?—every morning, feeling that way, like it was the first time?

And yet people came and called and cared and stayed. And each gesture came to feel almost miraculous to me. And there were moments when I would say, "You just don't know what this means to me."

And they didn't! They couldn't, or wouldn't. Isn't that wild? They really didn't see it. They really didn't recognize just how much their ordinary expressions of love would do for me.

On the one hand, I thought it was wonderful that they wouldn't make a big deal out of something that seemed so simple for them, just showing up. But on the other hand, I wanted to shake them, and say, "Do you know how beautiful you are! Won't you see?" As if they were angels who had forgotten.

~

In the incredible power of what seems such a simple act, we are reminded of what a precious gift we have received and can pass on. What we offer, and what can be welcomed with such gratitude and wonder, is a glimpse of our common divinity revealed in an ordinary act of kindness which any of us can perform.

Helping out is not some special skill. It is not the domain of rare individuals. It is not confined to a single part or time of our lives. We simply heed the call of that natural caring impulse within, and follow where it leads us.

~

I was a housewife and a mother, and when the kids got bigger, I was looking for something else to do. I wanted to give. But I had a good deal of self-doubt, not knowing really what I could do for anyone else, unsure of who I was, you might say.

But I was willing to try, and I see now that this was enough. Very often something just comes right in front of you. Like for me, it was an ad in the newspaper: "If you love animals, come volunteer at the Zoo." And it clicked, and I went, and I became a guide there.

We started an Outreach program, to bring animals to people who could never come to us. We'd bring them in twos—two birds, two mammals, two reptiles. The snake we'd show next to last. We'd end with a dove.

We'd take them to nursing homes, hospitals for incurable diseases, children's wards, burn units, mental hospitals. Places where people are very sick, or lost, or dying. They'll never go anyplace else again. They've lost interest, given up on life itself. I was very shocked by that; it hurt me.

But I witnessed things I'd never dreamed of when I answered that ad.

In one mental hospital we went to a group known as "the boys." "The boys" can be aged eighteen to forty-eight, but with a mental capability from infant to two or three years. They were constantly undressing, or urinating, naked as the day they were born. I had a ferret. One boy came running, yelling, "Touch! touch! touch!" I said, "You can touch him later." But when we got around to it, the feeling had left him. I just wanted to die. Tears streamed down my face. I'd missed it. Oh, did I miss it! But I've never missed it again.

In a cancer ward, a man refused to come out of his room. He was bitter and angry. Shame was in him. He heard there were animals so he was just a little curious. So this time, right away, I said, "Would you like to touch?" "Oh, sure, sure," he said sarcastically. "With these hands?" He thrust them in my face; there were no fingers left. Then he just looked down at the floor. I felt terrible, but I said, "Here, then—with your palms." And he began to let us help. With each animal he became softer. For once, there was something beside his illness. He began to cry. "This is so beautiful," he said. "I will never forget this." He became so warm.

A woman in a nursing home had been talking only nonsense for many, many years, as long as people could remember. She gabbed and played patty-cake. I had an opossum. I said, "They're really nature's garbage collectors." She looked up and said, "If that's the case, lady, you better tell them to join the union." She laughed and went back to patty-cake.

Working with snakes can be very powerful. They represent original sin and evil and death for many. Once, in a mental ward, we asked if we could show a snake; anyone could leave if they wanted to. They all agreed to stay. But when one man saw the snake, he began to wail and shriek. "This is evil, this is evil," he cried. "Shall we leave?" I asked. "No, let me try," he answered. He tried very hard. He began to touch, then scream, then touch, then scream. "Look," I finally said. "Say anything, but quietly. *You're* scaring the hell out of us." We spent five minutes of touch-and-scream. Then it was over. "Oh . . . " he said at the end, as he touched. "Oh, it feels so beautiful, the snake, it feels like gold." Horrible impressions all rolled up into serpents had gone out of him. Evil turned into gold. He had been healed of fear by the very animal that's supposed to have seduced us out of Eden.

It's just something to behold; it's as if you're in the presence of little miracles. To see another person feel the beauty of life. To see their pain transformed. To see an anguished face begin to soften. I never had been touched like this before.

All you're doing is coming in with help in your hands. It's not basically the animals even. It's something about life. The professionals notice that too. They get inspired. I've seen a few of them cry—cry for the patients, maybe for themselves, maybe at what they see happening. Their work is very hard, you know. I once noticed a doctor, holding some instruments, look at a bird in my hand. Then he looked at his instruments for a long time, it seemed. Then we looked at each other.

You couldn't pay me for what I get out of it. To think . . . just by answering an ad. You see, my childhood was very ugly. I was born in the wrong country at the wrong time with the wrong religion—a Jew in Germany during Hitler times. There was death all around. I was treated lower than the lowest animals. They could kill me anytime. We had no rights. Dogs had rights, but not Jews. We were exterminated, the way you exterminate insects. I was so very bitter for so very long. But I have learned compassion and forgiveness from what I have seen.

I was once in a criminal forensic unit in a mental institution. There you have what I considered animals, that did murders in the most gruesome way. I recognized some of them from the papers. Each of them I had condemned to death. They should be put in an electric chair. They should be eliminated.

But when I was in that unit, I learned a deep lesson. Here I was, face to face, enjoying life's creatures with human beings I had condemned to death. I looked around and said to myself, "Who are you to have condemned?" And suddenly I felt such forgiveness and understanding—for them, for myself, for everyone. For everyone.

So it has been a journey from fear and hate to love of all creation. Without question. And a journey of wonder, too—wonder in that I'm amazed, and wonder like I don't really understand it all, and how it's happened. I'm just grateful, to whoever or whatever is responsible for it all. Just very grateful.

~

Perhaps, finally, we can trust a little more—both ourselves and the process. We have much more to offer than we may realize. All we have to do is ask "How can I help?" with an open heart, and then really listen.

~

You ask yourself what helping is, or who helps, or what helps, and how much, and when are you, and when aren't you . . . and the whole conversation can get a little dizzy. What you're talking about is something you really understand instinctively, but the words can start to have a life of their own. Not that it isn't a wonderful topic. But there's always the potential for it all turning into the tea party in Alice in Wonderland.

I get evidence of this in a phone call one day. I am talking to a woman who is working for the Gallup poll. She's actually doing a poll on how much time people spend helping. She's trying to explain the criteria. I finally start to crack up, seeing something of the absurdity of it all.

"You all are crazy! 'How much time are people helping?' What kind of question is that? Tell Gallup he's nuts!"

She started to laugh as well. "I know. That's what I said too. What can I tell you? It's a job." She was sort of whispering, which made me laugh more. We got into this conspiratorial, infectious laughter at it all.

When we stopped laughing, I asked, "Was that helping?"

She said, "I guess so, sort of. Why was it?"

I said, "That's your *job. You tell* me *why." And then I threw in, "We were trying to make the best of a nutty situation. In fact, that's what I'm trying to do all the time. That's it—I want you to put me down in the Gallup poll as someone who helps all the time."*

More laughter. She said, "We don't have a category for 'All the Time.'"

"Oh ye of little faith."

"But we do have a line here that says, 'All of the Above.'"

(At this point I didn't know if she was kidding, but I went for it.) "Perfect. Put me down under 'All of the Above.' I am very All-of-the-Above. In fact, you have to put everybody down under 'All of the Above.' Everybody's trying to make the best of a nutty situation. Gallup can release a poll saying 'Everybody in America Is Helping.'"

"God," she said, "I wish I had the nerve. Maybe I'll do it with alternate answers. 'One Out of Every Two People in America Is Helping.' The other half is being helped."

By this point we were just in love with the idea of throwing the topic back into blessed confusion, which is where it really is anyhow. Finally, we said goodbye.

"It's been great," I said.

"Very helpful," she agreed.

Months later, there's a story in the newspaper: Gallup Poll Reveals Half of All Americans Help Out as Volunteers. Right there in the paper. She did it! She pulled it off!

I rush into the kitchen reading the headline to my wife. "That's me!" I exclaim.

"Which half?" says my very formidable and wonderful wife.

"All of the Above!" I answer triumphantly.

"Just wash the dishes," she replies.

~

Audiotapes, videos, and other books by Ram Dass are available from the Ram Dass Tape Library, 524 San Anselmo Avenue #203, San Anselmo, CA 94960. Write for a free catalog, or explore the web site at www.RamDassTapes.org.

A Note About the Authors

RAM DASS, a.k.a. Richard Alpert, received his Ph.D. in psychology from Stanford University and has taught at Harvard, Stanford, and the University of California. In the 1960s he was active in research on consciousness, with Timothy Leary, Aldous Huxley, Alan Watts, and others. In 1967 he continued his study of consciousness in India, where he was given the name Ram Dass (Servant of God) by his guru, Neem Karoli Baba. Since that time, through books, tapes, and lectures, he has contributed to the integration of Eastern spiritual philosophy into Western thought. In 1973 he founded the Hanuman Foundation, which has nurtured projects designed to increase spiritual consciousness in the West. Among these have been the Prison-Ashram Project, the Dying Project and Dying Center, and meditation programs and retreats. In 1985 he became the Chairman of the Board of the Seva Foundation. His primary "yoga" or vehicle for realizing liberation is through service.

PAUL GORMAN was educated at Yale and Oxford. He has been a program producer and talk show host with WBAI-FM, Pacifica Radio, in New York City, since 1969. He has worked as staff assistant to a group of Democratic congressmen and as consultant for the Senate Foreign Relations Committee. He served as Eugene McCarthy's press secretary and speechwriter in the 1968 presidential campaign, and has been an adviser to a number of public officials. He has taught at Sarah Lawrence College, The City University of New York, Adelphi University, Naropa Institute, and Omega Institute. He is presently Vice-President for Public Affairs and Advocacy at The Cathedral of St. John the Divine in New York City. He lives in The Cathedral Close with his wife, Enid, and daughter, Juliet.

A Note on the Type

This book was set in a digitized version of Baskerville. Designed by John Baskerville, the original face was the forerunner of the modern group of type faces.

John Baskerville (1706–1775), of Birmingham, England, was a writing master with a special renown for cutting inscriptions in stone. About 1750 he began experimenting with punch cutting and making typographical material, and in 1757 he published his first work, a Virgil in royal quarto, with great-primer letters; the types throughout had been designed by him. This was followed by his famous editions of Milton, the Bible, the Book of Common Prayer, and works by several Latin classical authors. His types, at first criticized as unnecessarily slender, delicate, and feminine, in time were recognized as both distinct and elegant, and his types as well as his printing were greatly admired.

Composed by American–Stratford Graphic Services, Inc.,
Brattleboro, Vermont.

Printed and bound by Fairfield Graphics,
Fairfield, Pennsylvania.

Designed by Iris Weinstein.